Knick-knacks for a pretty home

Annien Teubes

δελος

Cape Town

I am grateful to Him who controls everything in my life, to my family for their support and to Johann for his motivation.

Acknowledgements

DMC for all the embroidery cottons

For styling material:
Johan Taljaard for paintings
Vicky Street for clay pot
Elna and Lillibeth Slabber for their contributions
Horrockses for bed linen
Continental China for pottery
Baskets for All for baskets
Prima Toys for doll

© 1991 Delos
40 Heerengracht, Cape Town

Also available in Afrikaans as *Maak jou huis mooi*

Photography by Anton de Beer
Cover design by Mandie Smit
Typography by Corrine Lancaster
Translated by Elizé Lübbe
Typeset in 9.5 on 11 pt Bookman light by Unifoto, Cape Town
Printed and bound by Printkor, Cape Town

First edition, first impression 1991

ISBN 1-86826-140-9

General hints

Always use the best fabrics available, especially for articles that are used and washed frequently.

Make sure that the fabric is preshrunk and colourfast. This can be established by cutting a 10 cm square tester which is then washed and ironed. Now measure the tester to see if it has shrunk. The colour of the water will indicate if the colours have run.

Never use synthetic lace on cotton articles. Synthetic lace requires a cool iron, while cotton is usually ironed at a higher temperature which will cause the lace to melt.

It is important to remember that the amount of stretch may differ from fabric to fabric. Try to use fabrics with the same elasticity if more than one type of material is used for an article.

For appliqué all the pattern pieces must be cut on the same grain. If this is not done, the fabric will pucker giving the article an unattractive appearance.

Always use a good quality thread.

Both appliqué and decorative stitches will stand out and look very attractive if worked in machine embroidery thread. However, this is not essential and ordinary machine thread may be used if machine embroidery thread is not available.

It is essential to finish off articles properly to prevent seams from unravelling and to ensure the lifespan of the article.

A very convenient seam allowance, and one that will always be the same, is the width of the sewing machine foot. Measure your sewing to see if it is wide enough for the required seam allowance. The foot is usually 5-7 mm wide.

Contents

Colourful kitchens

*A kitchen looks particularly attractive if it is decorated in a
co-ordinated theme. Here are some ideas for a strawberry
theme in red, green and white as well as a duck
motif in shades of apricot and blue. Decorate kitchen towels,
tea cosies, tray cloths and pot-holders. Frame a
cross-stitch picture and make a shelf frill
with a cheerful strawberry motif.*

Cushion with embroidered strawberry motif

Materials

White cotton fabric for front: 37 cm square
White cotton fabric for back: 37 cm × 57 cm
Red-and-white polka dot fabric: 19 cm square
Thin white fabric to embroider: 15 cm square
DMC stranded embroidery cotton: 1 skein each Blanc,
  913, 910, 742, 745, 762, 321 and 310
Red-and-white striped cotton fabric for frill: 2,6 m ×
  8 cm
Green and white machine embroidery thread
Red and white sewing thread
6,5 cm wide white lace: 1,5 m
Embroidery frame
Embroidery needle
Tracing paper

Method

○ Transfer the embroidery diagram (Pattern 1 on p. 56)
  onto the 15 cm square of white fabric.
○ Place the fabric in an embroidery frame and complete the embroidery according to the diagram. Use
  long-and-short stitch for the strawberries, stem
  stitch for the stalks, satin stitch for the leaves and the
  dots on the strawberries and French knots for the
  flower centres. Outline the strawberries in black stem
  stitch. The lines on the diagram indicate the direction of the stitches.
○ Work all loose threads to the back and press lightly on
  the wrong side.
○ Place the red-and-white polka dot fabric in the centre
  of the white cotton fabric for the front of the cushion
  (Sketch 1a, point 2) and zigzag in place.
○ Cut a circle with a diameter of 14 cm from the embroidered fabric (Sketch 1a, point 1).
○ Position the embroidered circle in the centre of the
  red-and-white polka dot fabric and stitch in place
  with a row of dense satin stitches in white thread
  (Sketch 1a, point 6).
○ Work a decorative stitch in green machine embroidery thread just inside the edge of the circle (Sketch
  1a, point 3).
○ Neatly stitch the white lace around the red-and-white
  polka dot fabric (Sketch 1a, point 5).
○ Finish off one raw edge of the frill, fold over a 0,5 cm
  hem and stitch in place.
○ Gather the other raw edge to fit around the front of the
  cushion.
○ Join the two ends of the frill and, with right sides facing, stitch it to the front (Sketch 1a, point 7).
○ Divide the back of the cover into two equal sections,
  each 37 cm × 28,5 cm. Finish off one 37 cm raw edge
  on each section. Fold over a 1 cm hem along these
  edges and stitch (Sketch 1b, point 8).
○ Place one back section on the front with right sides
  facing the frill in between and the hem in the centre.
  Stitch around the raw edges (Sketch 1b, point 9).
  Repeat with the second back section.

○ Finish off the four raw edges and turn the cover to the
  right side.
○ Press the seams lightly and place a cushion inside
  the cover. A green satin bow may be sewn onto the
  front (Sketch 1a, point 4).

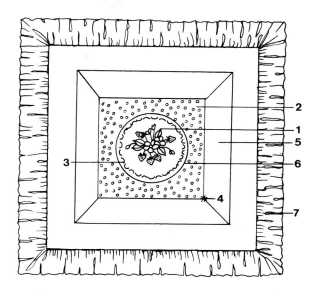

Sketch 1a

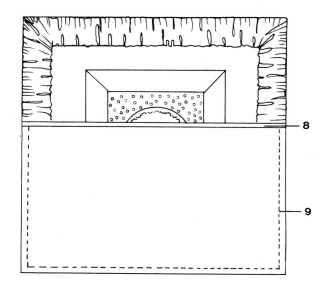

Sketch 1b

5

Smocked cushion

Materials

Red-and-white striped cotton fabric for front: 36 cm ×
    33 cm
White cotton fabric for back: 36 cm × 53 cm
Red-and-white polka dot fabric: 60 cm × 6 cm
White fabric for smocking: about 60 cm × 20 cm (com-
    pleted size: 11 cm × 7 cm)
6 mm wide green satin ribbon: 110 cm
2 cm wide white lace: 60 cm
6 cm wide white lace: 2,2 m
DMC stranded embroidery cotton for smocking: 1 skein
    each 321 and 911
White sewing thread
Wadding: 11 cm × 7 cm

Method

○ If you are unfamiliar with the smocking technique,
  you will have to consult an embroidery guide for the
  stitch methods. Embroider the strawberries according to Sketch 2a on smocking fabric.
○ With right side up, place the red-and-white striped
  cotton fabric on the work surface. Cut the wadding to
  the correct size and place it in the centre of the striped
  fabric. Place the smocked fabric on the wadding with
  the right side up. Carefully pin and tack all three
  layers together. Make sure that the pleats of the
  smocked fabric are straight. Stitch the smocked
  fabric neatly in place.
○ Divide the long strip of red-and-white polka dot fabric
  into four sections and stitch it around the smocked
  section as shown in Sketch 2b. Points 1-4 show the
  sequence in which the strips must be stitched. Use a
  straight stitch to stitch the outer edges of the four
  strips (Sketch 2b, point 5).

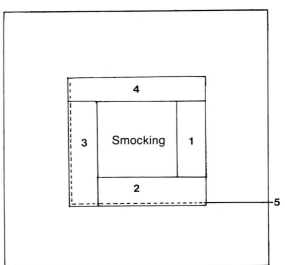

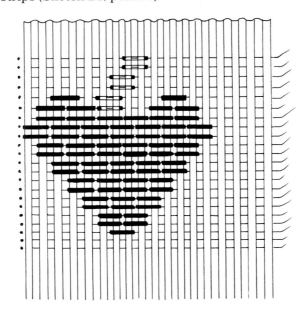

Sketch 2a

Sketch 2b

- Stitch the narrow white lace around the smocking (Sketch 2c, point 6). Work all the threads through to the wrong side and neaten.
- Work a dense row of satin stitch along the inside edge of the lace (Sketch 2c, point 7).
- Using a criss-cross stitch, stitch the green satin ribbon onto the outer edge of the polka dot strips (Sketch 2c, point 8).
- Tie the remaining ribbon into a bow and sew in place as shown in Sketch 2c, point 9.
- Gather the wide white lace to fit around the front of the cushion.
- Join the two ends of the lace and, right sides facing, stitch the gathered lace onto the front (Sketch 2c, point 10).
- Divide the back of the cover into two equal sections, each 36 cm × 26,5 cm.
- Finish off one 36 cm raw edge on each piece. Fold over a 1 cm hem along these edges and stitch (Sketch 2d, point 11).
- Place one back section on the front with right sides facing and the hem in the centre. Stitch around the raw edges (Sketch 2d, point 12). Repeat with the second back section.
- Finish off the four raw edges and turn the cover to the right side.
- Press the seams lightly and place a cushion inside the cover.

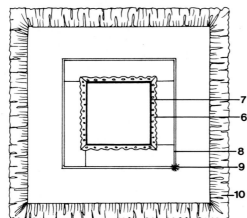

Sketch 2c

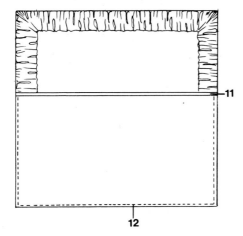

Sketch 2d

Tray cloth with strawberry appliqué

Materials

White cotton fabric: 45 cm × 30 cm
Red fabric for strawberry: 8 cm square
Red-and-white polka dot fabric: 8 cm square
Green fabric for leaves: 10 cm square
5 cm wide white cotton anglaise lace: 2,4 m
6 mm wide red satin ribbon: 1,6 m
Red and green DMC machine embroidery thread
Red sewing thread
Tissue paper
Tracing paper

Method

- Cut out the tray cloth according to Pattern 2 on p. 57. Note that the pattern is placed 2 cm from the fold line of the fabric which will make the tray cloth 4 cm wider.
- Cut out the strawberries from the green, red and red-and-white polka dot fabric. Note that the grain of the strawberries must match that of the tray cloth. The strawberry pattern must therefore be cut on the cross so that the grain will eventually be straight when the strawberry is appliquéd at an angle.
- Neatly finish off the raw edges of the tray cloth.
- Place tissue paper under the fabric and pin the strawberries and leaves in position (Sketch 3, point 1).
- Tack and then stitch in place using a dense satin stitch and the green and the red machine embroidery thread.
- Work all loose threads to the wrong side and neaten securely. This is particularly important as the article will be washed frequently.
- Gather the white lace evenly so that it fits around the outer edge of the tray cloth.
- Join the ends with a French seam and stitch the lace along the edge of the tray cloth (Sketch 3, point 2).
- Using criss-cross stitch, stitch the red satin ribbon onto the row of stitches around the lace (Sketch 3, point 3)
- Finish off with a row of decorative stitches in green, 0,5 cm from the satin ribbon (Sketch 3, point 4).
- Press the tray cloth neatly and enjoy your handiwork.

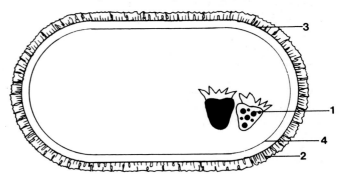

Sketch 3

8

Red tea cosy with strawberry appliqué

Materials

Red fabric: 2 pieces, each 25 cm × 30 cm; 1 piece 64 cm
  × 8 cm for gusset
Lining: 2 pieces, each 25 cm × 30 cm; 1 piece 64 cm
  × 8 cm for gusset
Wadding: 2 pieces, each 25 cm × 30 cm; 1 piece 64 cm
  × 8 cm for gusset
3,5 cm wide white cotton anglaise lace: 1,05 m
Red-and-white polka dot fabric for 3 strawberries
Green fabric for leaves
Red, white and green machine embroidery thread
Red sewing thread
Tissue paper
Tracing paper

Method

○ Use Pattern 3 on p. 58 to cut out the sections for the
  tea cosy from the red fabric, lining and wadding.
○ Use pattern 4 on p. 58 to cut 3 strawberries from the
  green fabric and the red-and-white polka dot fabric.
  Remember to cut out the strawberries in such a way
  that the grain is the same as that of the backing fabric
  once they are stitched in place.
○ Tack the strawberries and leaves onto the red front of
  the tea cosy (Sketch 4, point 1).
○ Place the tissue paper under the red fabric and stitch
  all the appliqué pieces in place using a dense satin
  stitch and machine embroidery thread – green
  around the leaves and white around the strawberries.
  The tissue paper helps to keep the fabric taut and
  prevents the stitches puckering.
○ Work all loose threads to the wrong side and neaten.
○ Place the layers of each of the front, back and gusset
  together as follows: first the lining, then the wadding
  and lastly the red fabric.
○ Place the three layers of the appliquéd front in front of
  you with the right side up.

○ Gather the cotton anglaise lace (Sketch 4, point 2) to
  fit between the two points shown in Pattern 3. Stitch
  the lace frill in place between the two points.
○ Stitch a row of dense satin stitches in green thread
  just inside the lace frill (Sketch 4, point 3).
○ Using red machine embroidery thread, work a row of
  double action straight stitches 1 cm from the green
  stitches. Repeat 0,5 cm from the first row and again
  0,5 cm from the second (Sketch 4, point 4).
○ Finish off the raw edges of all three layers of both the
  back and the gusset together.
○ With right sides facing, pin the gusset to the front.
  Join the seam.
○ The back of the tea cosy is now stitched to the gusset
  in the same way.
○ Finish off the two seams together on the wrong side.
○ Trim the bottom edges evenly and finish off with a
  row of dense satin stiches in red thread (Sketch 4,
  point 5).

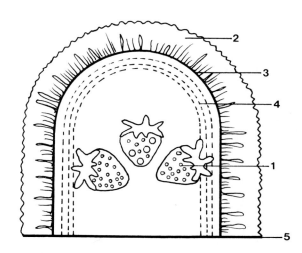

Sketch 4

9

Quilted tray cloth

This is a very useful tray cloth which is also thick enough to be used as a place mat. Use matching remnants and remember to vary the width of the strips.

Materials

Red fabric: 8 cm × 30 cm
Red fabric: 5 cm × 30 cm
Red fabric with white polka dots: 9 cm × 30 cm
White fabric with red polka dots: 5 cm × 30 cm
Red fabric with large red polka dots: 6 cm × 30 cm
Red fabric with white hearts: 7,5 cm × 30 cm
Red-and-white striped fabric: 8,5 cm × 30 cm
Red fabric with white flowers: 5,5 cm × 30 cm
5 cm wide white cotton lace: 2,4 m
Red machine embroidery thread
Wadding: 48 cm × 30 cm
Lining: 48 cm × 30 cm
Tracing paper

Method

○ Stitch the strips together as follows (see Sketch 5a): point 1 – red fabric 5 cm wide; point 2 – red fabric with white polka dots; point 3 – white fabric with red polka dots; point 4 – red fabric 8 cm wide; point 5 – red fabric with large red polka dots; point 6 – red fabric with white flowers; point 7 – red-and-white striped fabric; point 8 – red fabric with white hearts.
○ Press all seams open.
○ Place the wadding between the lining and the upper patchwork layer which has its right side facing up.
○ Pin the three layers together securely and tack through all three layers.
○ Using red machine embroidery thread and a double action straight stitch, stitch 7 mm inside every seam (Sketch 5b, point 9). Make sure that the upper layer and the lining are lying smoothly before stitching.
○ Fold the completed patchwork fabric in half. Use Pattern 2 on p. 57 and place it 2 cm from the fold line of the fabric (Sketch 5c, point 10).
○ Making sure that the pattern is straight, cut out the tray cloth.
○ Gather the white cotton lace evenly to fit around the edge of the tray cloth. Join the two ends with a French seam. This will prevent the seam from fraying if it is washed frequently.
○ With right sides facing, place the lace along the edge of the tray cloth and stitch in place (Sketch 5d, point 11).
○ Finish off the raw edges of the tray cloth and the lace together, fold the lace back and press.
○ Topstitch on the right side to prevent the lace folding back (Sketch 5e, point 12).
○ Press the tray cloth and it is ready for use.

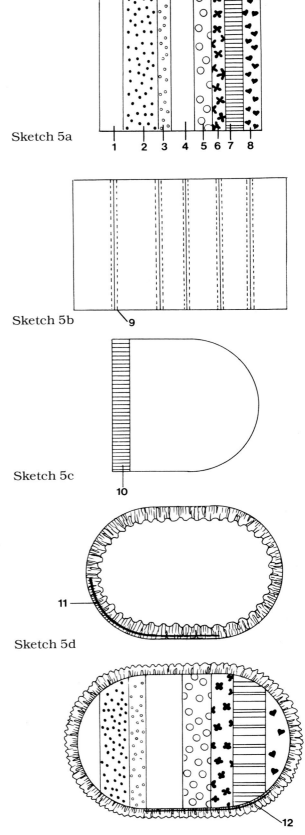

Sketch 5a

Sketch 5b

Sketch 5c

Sketch 5d

Sketch 5e

Strawberry pot-holder

Materials

Red fabric for back of strawberry: 20 cm × 22 cm
Red fabric with white polka dots for front of strawberry:
   20 cm × 22 cm
Green fabric for front and back of leaves: 20 cm × 30 cm
Thick wadding: 20 cm × 52 cm
6 mm wide green satin ribbon: 10 cm
Green machine embroidery thread
Green and red sewing thread
Tissue paper
Tracing paper

Method

○ Use Pattern 5a on p. 59 to cut one strawberry from the plain red fabric and one from the red-and-white polka dot fabric. Make sure the pattern markings correspond with the grain of the fabric.
○ Cut another strawberry from the wadding.
○ Place the wadding (Sketch 6a, point 2) on the tissue paper (Sketch 6a, point 1). Place the fabric strawberries with right sides together on top of the wadding (Sketch 6a, point 3).
○ Baste through all four layers, but remember to leave an opening for turning the strawberry to the right side (Sketch 6a, point 4).
○ Stitch a seam 7 mm from the edge of the strawberry (Sketch 6a, point 5) leaving an opening for turning.
○ Remove the tissue paper. Trim the seam allowance and make a few clips at the curves. Turn the strawberry to the right side.
○ Fold in the raw edge at the opening and tack to close.
○ Using a straight stitch, stitch 2 mm from the edge of the strawberry (Sketch 6b, point 6).
○ Fold the green fabric into two equal sections, each 20 cm × 15 cm. Use Pattern 5b on p. 60 to cut out two leaves. Cut out another from the wadding.
○ Place the wadding between the two pieces of green fabric and tack the three layers together.
○ Fold the satin ribbon in half, insert it where indicated (Sketch 6b, point 7) and then finish off all three layers of the leaf together with a row of dense satin stitches in green thread (Sketch 6b, point 8).
○ Stitch the leaf onto the strawberry. Use green machine embroidery thread and a straight stitch directly next to the satin stitch (Sketch 6b, point 9).

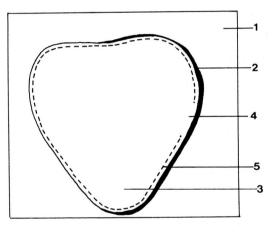

Sketch 6a

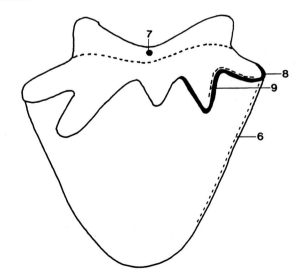

Sketch 6b

Kitchen towel with fabric border

Materials

1 red towel: 30 cm × 57 cm
Red-and-white printed cotton fabric: 8 cm × 32 cm
6 mm wide green satin ribbon: 64 cm
Green and white sewing thread

Method

○ Finish off the raw edges on the fabric strip.
○ Press the strip and fold over a 1 cm hem on both the short sides.
○ Tack the finished strip onto the right side of the towel, 5 cm from the edge. Make sure that the strip is lying straight (Sketch 7, point 1).
○ Use a straight stitch to sew the fabric strip to the towel.
○ Divide the satin ribbon into two lengths of 32 cm each. Fold over 1 cm at both ends of each ribbon.
○ Using green sewing thread and criss-cross stitch, stitch the satin ribbon onto each edge of the fabric strip (Sketch 7, point 2 and 3).
○ Finish off all loose threads securely.

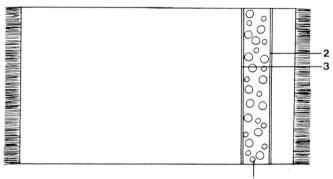

Sketch 7

Kitchen towel with cross-stitch border

Materials

Red towel: 30 cm × 57 cm
White cross-stitch fabric strip: 32 cm
White sewing thread
DMC stranded embroidery cotton: 1 skein each Blanc, 321, 745, 702, 700 and 310

Method

○ Follow the embroidery diagram (Sketch 8) to embroider the cross-stitch motif in the centre of the strip (57 stitches × 8 stitches).
○ Fold over a 1 cm hem on both raw edges.
○ Tack the embroidered strip onto the towel, 3,5 cm from the edge.
○ Use a straight stitch to sew the strip to the towel.
○ Press the strip flat and show off your handiwork.

Hint: Cross-stitch fabric strips can be bought in different widths. In this case a strip of 8-count fabric was used. However, the pattern may also be used on wider strips. Just see to it that, if possible, an equal number of stitch spaces are left above and below the motif.

	DMC-no.
W	Blanc
—	321
■	745
s	702
o	700

Black outlining with 1 strand 310

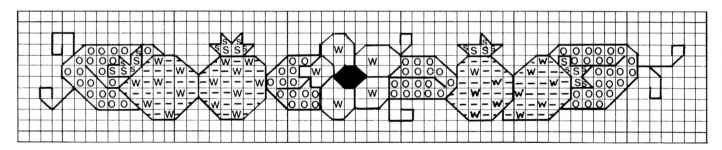

Sketch 8

Appliquéd jam jar covers

Materials

For 3 jam jar lids, diameter of lid 10 cm:
White cotton fabric: 60 cm × 20 cm
Scraps of red and green fabric
Green and red machine embroidery thread
White and brown sewing thread
4 cm wide white cotton anglaise lace: 2,5 m
Tissue paper
6 mm wide satin ribbon: 60 cm
Tracing paper

Method

○ Draw a circle with a diameter of 15,3 cm on paper and cut out the pattern.
○ Use to cut three circles from the white cotton fabric.
○ Use Pattern 6 on p. 60 to cut out the apple, cherry and strawberry from the red and green fabric. The fabric must be neatly pressed, otherwise the appliqué will look untidy.
○ Place the white cotton circle, right side up, onto a piece of tissue paper.
○ Pin the apple and two leaves in position and tack neatly.
○ Using a straight stitch, stitch around the motifs 1 mm from the edge. This will prevent creases when the satin stitch is done.
○ Use machine embroidery thread and finish off the motifs with a row of dense satin stitches – red around the apple and green around the leaves.
○ Work all loose threads through to the wrong side and neaten.
○ Finish off the raw edge of the cotton circle.
○ Divide the white anglaise lace into three equal lengths. Join the two ends on one length with a French seam and gather so that it fits exactly around the circle.
○ Stitch the lace around the edge of the circle using criss-cross stitch.
○ Press the article and place it on a suitable container. Place an elastic band around the lid and tie a satin bow over the elastic.
○ The cherry and strawberry jam jar covers are made in the same way. Use brown sewing thread to stitch the stems of the cherries.

Hint: Any 4 cm wide lace may be stitched around the cover, but try to use lace that has two finished edges, otherwise there could be a problem with the unfinished raw edge.

Small patterned jam jar covers

Materials

For 1 jam jar lid with a diameter of 7 cm:
Patterned cotton remnant: 16 cm square
2 cm wide matching cotton lace: 70 cm
Matching sewing thread
6 mm wide satin ribbon: 45 cm
Tracing paper

Method

○ Draw a circle with a diameter of 14,5 cm on paper and cut out to use as a pattern.
○ Cut the circle from the patterned cotton fabric.
○ Finish off the raw edge.
○ Join the two ends of the lace and gather so that it fits exactly around the circle.
○ Using criss-cross stitch, stitch the gathered lace onto the circle.
○ Press neatly. Place the cover on the lid. Place an elastic band around the lid, tie a piece of satin ribbon over the elastic and the jar is ready to take pride of place on your shelf.

Framed card

All of us have from time to time cast about for something to brighten up the kitchen (or any other room). However, take time to look around before you delve deep into your pocket to buy that "something".

It is not always necessary to buy the most expensive picture or print. The same effect can be obtained if a suitable card that looks "different" is framed attractively.

The picture of a basket of strawberries was cut out carefully and glued onto a white mount. Green and red mounts were used around it and the cheerful picture was finished off with a narrow wooden frame (see photo on p. 8).

Framed cross-stitch picture

The strawberry theme can be continued in the kitchen with a framed picture in cross-stitch. Embroider the little girl with the strawberries and see the difference it makes to that blank spot on the wall. The picture can also be used in a child's bedroom.

Materials

14-count Aïda cross-stitch fabric
DMC stranded embroidery cotton: 1 skein each white, black, ecru, 744, 368, 909, 838, 841, 321, 814, 225, 224, 322, 310, 223, 334, 3045 and 738. Two skeins 775
Embroidery needle
Embroidery frame

Method

○ Cut the cross-stitch fabric to the size of the picture plus a 4 cm border all around. In order to frame the picture properly, it is important to leave ample fabric around the edge.
○ Zigzag the raw edges. If you do not have a sewing machine, use masking tape to prevent the edges from fraying.
○ Find the centre of the fabric as follows: Fold the fabric in half to establish the centre of the side. Use ordinary machine thread and sew a tacking stitch over each cross-stitch sized square across the length of the material. Do the same with the width. The intersection of these two lines is the centre point. Start embroidering here and complete the motif according to the embroidery diagram in Sketch 9.
○ Press the completed article on the wrong side with a hot iron and a damp cloth.
○ Have the completed picture framed.

Strawberry shelf frill

Materials

White cotton fabric: 15 cm × length of shelf
Red cotton fabric with white polka dots: 10 cm × length of shelf + 15 cm
Green cotton fabric: 6 cm × length of shelf + 15 cm
Red and green machine embroidery thread
Ordinary white sewing thread
Tracing paper

Method

○ Finish off all the raw edges of the white fabric strip to prevent it fraying while it is being handled.
○ Use Pattern 7a and 7b on p. 61 to trace a pattern for the strawberry and the leaf onto paper.
○ Fold over one end of the red-and-white polka dot fabric strip to the width of the strawberry. Place the fold line of the pattern on the fold of the fabric and cut out. Continue cutting joined pairs of strawberries un-

til there are enough for the length of the shelf (Sketch 10a).
○ Cut out the leaves from the green fabric in the same way.
○ The number of strawberries required can be established beforehand by dividing the length of the shelf by the width of the strawberry (8,5 cm). If the strawberries don't fit exactly, two equal lengths of white fabric may be left at the ends, or the strawberries and leaves can overlap slightly.
○ Fold over 1 cm of the top edge of the white fabric strip and stitch the narrow hem.
○ Place the strawberries next to each other on the white fabric with their points on the bottom edge of the strip. Tack in place (Sketch 10b, point 1).
○ Place the leaves along the top of the strawberries with the edges overlapping and tack in place (Sketch 10b, point 2).
○ Use red machine embroidery thread to stitch a row of dense satin stitches around the edge of the strawberries.
○ Trim away excess white fabric below the strawberries. Cut close to the stitching, but be careful not to cut into it (Sketch 10b, point 3).

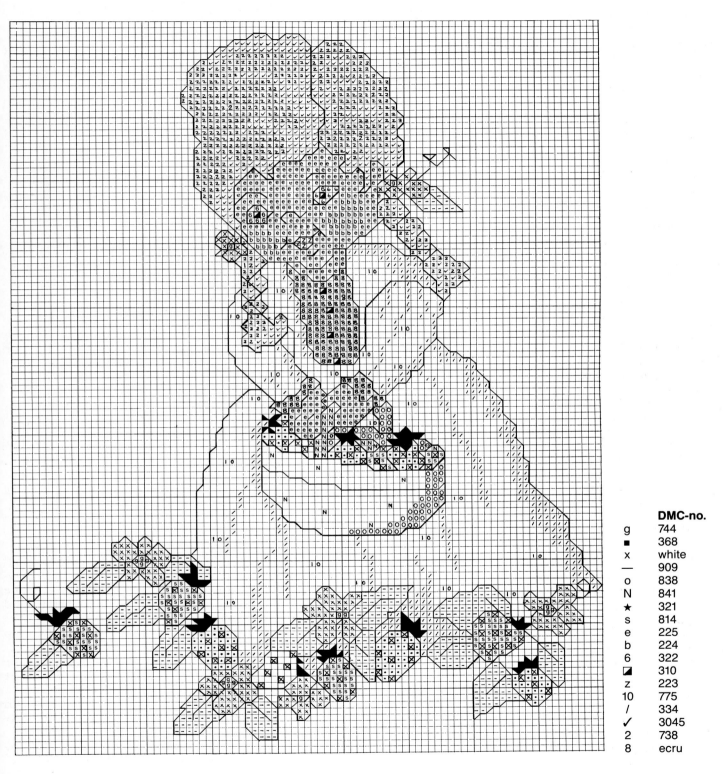

	DMC-no.
g	744
■	368
x	white
—	909
o	838
N	841
★	321
s	814
e	225
b	224
6	322
◤	310
z	223
10	775
/	334
✓	3045
2	738
8	ecru

Size: 89 stitches wide × 111 stitches high
Outline all sections with one strand of black

Sketch 9

- Use green machine embroidery thread to work a row of dense satin stitches around the edge of the leaves. Work all loose threads to the wrong side and neaten.
- Finish off the shelf frill by folding over a narrow hem in the sides of the white fabric and stitching it in place.
- The shelf frill may be starched if desired.

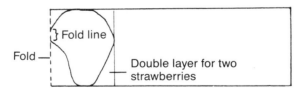

Sketch 10a

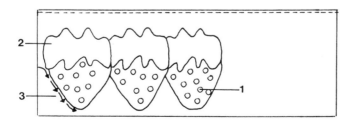

Sketch 10b

Mixer cover

Measurements: width 42 cm; height 28 cm; depth 16 cm

Compare the measurements of your mixer with those given above before cutting the pattern. If they differ, you may still follow the step-by-step directions, but the measurements of the pattern will have to be adjusted.

Materials

Floral cotton fabric for front and back: 2 pieces, each 44 cm × 31 cm (42 cm + 2 cm × 28 cm + 3 cm)
Lining for front and back: 2 pieces, each 44 cm × 31 cm
Thin foam rubber for front and back: 2 pieces, each 44 cm × 31 cm
Floral cotton fabric for gusset: 106 cm × 18 cm
Lining for gusset: 106 cm × 18 cm
Thin foam rubber for gusset: 106 cm × 18 cm
Blue fabric for frill: 11 cm × 2,5 m
Blue fabric for two ducks: 30 cm square
Apricot fabric for beaks and feet: 20 cm × 5 cm
2,5 cm wide apricot satin ribbon: 1 m
Blue and apricot machine embroidery thread

16

Blue sewing thread
2 wobbly eyes, about 1 cm in diameter
Glue stick
Tissue paper
Tracing paper

Method

○ Draw the pattern for the gusset, the front and the back onto paper according to the measurements given above.
○ Trace Pattern 8 on p. 61 for the duck onto paper.
○ Cut the front, back and gusset from each of the following: floral cotton fabric, thin foam rubber and lining.
○ Cut two ducks from the blue fabric and two beaks and two of each foot pattern from the apricot fabric.
○ Place the two ducks facing each other, more or less in the centre of the floral front. Pin the bodies in position and do the same with the beaks and feet. Now glue the pieces down carefully using the glue stick. However, do not use too much glue, as it may cause lumps under the fabric.
○ Carefully work a row of straight stitches around the outer edges of the ducks (Sketch 11a, point 1).
○ Place a layer of tissue paper underneath the fabric and stitch a row of dense satin stitches around the ducks using the machine embroidery thread. First stitch around the feet and beaks and then around the bodies. Use the apricot thread for the feet and beaks and the blue thread for the bodies.
○ Press the appliqué and sew the two wobbly eyes in position (Sketch 11a, point 2).
○ Divide the satin ribbon into two 50 cm lengths, tie each into a bow and sew the bows at an angle onto the neck of each duck (Sketch 11a, point 3).
○ Place all three layers of the front together, with the foam rubber in between the cotton fabric and the lining, and finish off the raw edges together. Do the same with the gusset and the back.
○ With right sides facing, fold the fabric for the frill in half lengthways and stitch the two short sides (Sketch 11c, point 1).
○ Turn the frill to the right side. Press the side seams and iron the fold line flat. Gather the frill to fit between the two points indicated (Sketch 11a, point 4).
○ Place the frill on the right side of the front and stitch in place (Sketch 11b, point 1).
○ With right sides facing, tack the gusset to the front with the frill in between. Clip the gusset 5 cm on either side of the top corners to make the fabric fit neatly around the corners. Stitch.
○ With right sides facing, tack the back to the gusset and stitch. Remember once again to clip the corners of the gusset on either side.

- Carefully press the seams open, ensuring that the frill stands up nicely.
- Fold over a 2 cm hem at the bottom edge and stitch in place. The bottom edge may also be finished off with bias binding.

> **Hint:** The dotted lines on the pattern indicate how much of the fabric of the beaks and feet must be inserted under the body fabric to prevent gaps between the pieces.

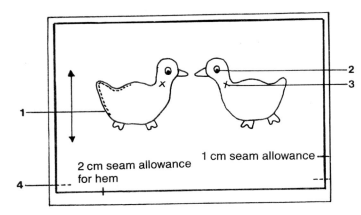

Sketch 11a

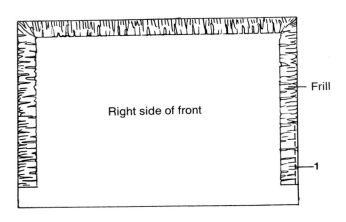

Sketch 11b

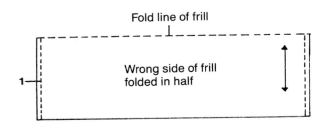

Sketch 11c

18

Toaster cover

Measurements: width 42 cm; height 28 cm; depth 16 cm

Compare the measurements of your toaster with those given above before cutting the pattern. If they differ, you may still follow the step-by-step directions, but the measurements of the pattern will have to be adjusted.

Materials

Floral cotton fabric for front and back: 2 pieces, each 34 cm × 24 cm (32 cm + 2 cm × 21 cm + 3 cm)
Lining for front and back: 2 pieces, each 34 cm × 24 cm
Thin foam rubber for front and back: 2 pieces, each 34 cm × 24 cm
Floral cotton fabric for gusset: 82 cm × 15 cm
Lining for gusset: 82 cm × 15 cm
Thin foam rubber for gusset: 82 cm × 15 cm
Blue fabric for frill: 10 cm × 1,9 m
Blue bias binding: 1 m
2,5 mm wide apricot satin ribbon: 50 cm
1 wobbly eye with a diameter of about 1 cm
Blue fabric for duck: 15 cm square
Apricot fabric for beak and feet: 10 cm × 5 cm
Blue and apricot machine embroidery thread
Blue sewing thread
Glue stick
Tissue paper
Tracing paper

Method

- Draw the pattern for the gusset, the front and the back onto paper according to the measurements given above.
- Trace Pattern 8 on p. 61 for the duck onto paper.
- Cut the front, back and gusset from each of the following: floral cotton fabric, thin foam rubber and lining.
- Cut a duck from the blue fabric and the beak and feet from the apricot fabric.
- Place the duck facing left, more or less in the centre of the floral front. Pin the body in position and do the same with the beak and feet. Now glue the pieces down carefully using the glue stick. However, do not use too much glue, as it may cause lumps under the fabric.
- Carefully work a row of straight stitches around the outer edges of the duck (Sketch 11a, point 1).
- Place a layer of tissue paper underneath the fabric and stitch a row of dense satin stitches around the pattern pieces using the machine embroidery thread. First stitch around the feet and beak and then around the body. Use the apricot thread for the feet and beak and blue thread for the body.
- Press the appliqué and sew the wobbly eye in position (Sketch 11a, point 2).
- Tie the satin ribbon into a bow and sew at a slight angle onto the duck's neck (Sketch 11a, point 3).
- Place all three layers of the front together, with the

19

foam rubber in between the cotton fabric and the lining, and finish off the raw edges together. Do the same with the gusset and the back.

○ With right sides facing, fold the fabric for the frill in half lengthways and stitch the two short sides (Sketch 11c, point 1).

○ Turn the frill to the right side. Press the side seams and iron the fold line flat. Gather the frill to fit between the two points indicated (Sketch 11a, point 4).

○ Place the frill on the right side of the front and stitch in place (Sketch 11b, point 1).

○ With right sides facing, tack the gusset to the front with the frill in between. Clip the gusset 5 cm on either side of the top corners to make the fabric fit neatly around the corners. Stitch.

○ With right sides facing, tack the back to the gusset and stitch. Remember once again to clip the corners of the gusset on either side.

○ Carefully press the seams open, ensuring that the frill stands up nicely.

○ Trim the bottom edges evenly and finish them off with blue bias binding.

Quilted place mat with appliquéd motif and matching napkin

Materials

For 1 place mat and 1 napkin:
Floral cotton fabric for place mat: 50 cm × 34 cm
Thin foam rubber for place mat: 50 × 34 cm
Lining for place mat: 50 cm × 34 cm
Matching cut-out flower for appliqué: about 16 cm × 15 cm
Apricot fabric for napkin: 36 cm square
4 cm wide cream lace: 2,85 m
Blue, green and apricot machine embroidery thread
Cream sewing thread
Tissue paper
Tracing paper

Method

○ Cut the cotton fabric, lining and foam for the place mat 50 cm × 34 cm.

○ Place all three layers together with the right sides of the top layer and the lining facing outward and the foam in between (Sketch 12a, points 1, 2 and 3).

○ Pin and tack through all three layers (Sketch 12a, points 4 and 5).

○ Using blue or apricot machine embroidery thread, work rows of criss-cross stitches 2,5 cm apart across the length and breadth of the fabric to form 2,5 cm squares (Sketch 12b, point 1).

○ Use pattern 2 on p. 57 to cut out the place mat. Remember to place the fold line of the pattern 2 cm from the fold of the fabric to make the place mat 4 cm wider.

○ Cut out the fabric according to the pattern and finish off the raw edges.

○ Place the cut-out flower on tissue paper and stitch around the edge, using a dense satin stitch in green and apricot machine embroidery thread. Work all loose threads to the wrong side and neaten.

○ Positioning the finished flower on the left-hand side of the place mat, stitch the top and bottom using straight stitch. The sides are left open so that the napkin can be inserted through the opening (Sketch 12c, point 1).

○ Slightly round the corners on the napkin and finish off the outer edge with a row of satin stitches in apricot machine embroidery thread.

○ Work a row of decorative stitches with blue machine embroidery thread about 1 cm inside the finished edge.

○ Gather or pleat the cream lace until it fits around the place mat. Join the ends of the lace very neatly, because an untidy join will spoil an otherwise neatly finished article.

○ Stitch the lace around the place mat with zigzag or criss-cross stitch.

> **Hint:** This quilted place mat and matching napkin are ideal for your guest's breakfast tray. They look neat and are pretty enough to whet anyone's appetite.

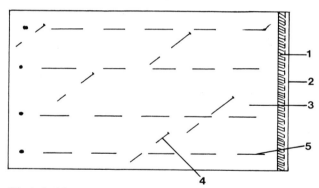

Sketch 12a

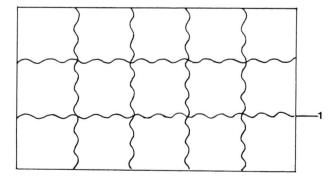

Sketch 12b

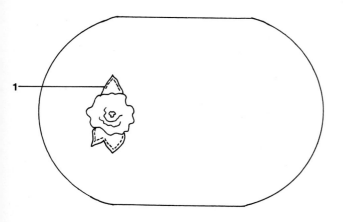

1

Sketch 12c

Jar covers for jam cruet

Materials

For 3 jar covers:
Blue, apricot and floral cotton fabric: 1 piece of each,
   each 15 cm square
1 cm wide pregathered apricot lace: 1,2 m
6 mm wide apricot satin ribbon: 3 lengths of 40 cm each

Apricot sewing thread
3 elastic bands
6 mm wide apricot satin ribbon: 45 cm
Paper

Method

○ Draw a circle with a diameter of 12 cm on the paper to
  use as a pattern.
○ Cut out a circle from each of the three fabrics.
○ Finish off the raw edge on each circle.
○ Divide the lace into three equal lengths. Shape the
  lace to fit around the circle and join the ends.
○ Stitch the lace around each circle. Fold a few pleats at
  equal distances so that the lace will fit neatly and to
  prevent the fabric puckering.
○ Press neatly.
○ Place the covers over the jars and secure with elastic
  bands.
○ Divide the apricot satin ribbon into three equal
  lengths and tie in bows over the elastic bands.

Hint: The covers are small, otherwise very little of
the jam jars will be visible. Use a circle with a diameter of 14 cm if you prefer larger covers. Remember
that you will then need more lace.

Cosy dining nooks

*When you decorate your diningroom, choose colour combinations
that tone in with the rest of the decor. Here are a
few ideas for dining nooks with matching tablecloths,
place mats, napkins, tea cosies and pot-holders
in elegant blue, burgundy and cream or
with a cosy cottagey effect
in pink and cream.*

Patchwork place mats with matching napkins

Materials

For 1 place mat and 1 napkin:
Dark blue cotton fabric: 33 cm × 9,5 cm
Striped burgundy and cream cotton fabric: 2 strips,
   each 33 cm × 9,5 cm
Burgundy cotton fabric: 2 strips, each 33 cm × 9,5 cm
Wadding or thin foam rubber: 33 cm × 43 cm
Lining, e.g., preshrunk unbleached linen: 33 cm ×
   43 cm
Dark blue bias binding: 1,25 m
Burgundy fabric for napkin: 36 cm square
Blue machine embroidery thread
Blue sewing thread
Tracing paper

Method

○ Join the five strips of fabric as follows: 1 – burgundy,
   2 – striped, 3 – dark blue, 4 – striped and 5 – burgundy (Sketch 13, points 1-5).
○ With right sides facing, stitch the burgundy and
   striped strips together, allowing a 0,5 cm seam.
○ Repeat with all five strips and then neatly press the
   seams open.
○ Use Pattern 9 on p. 62 to cut out the place mat pattern
   from paper.
○ Place the joined strips on the lining, with right sides
   up, and place the wadding or thin foam in between.
   Pin the pattern to the three layers of fabric (Sketch 13,
   points 6, 7 and 8).
○ Cut the layers according to the pattern, making sure
   that the dark blue strip is exactly in the centre.
○ Finish off the edges of the three layers together.
○ Finish off the edge with blue bias binding. Join the
   ends neatly.
○ Neaten all loose threads and press the place mat.
○ Finish off the edge of the burgundy napkin using a
   row of dense satin stitches in blue thread.
○ Neaten the threads at the corners and make sure the
   corners are not too bulky.
○ If you have an overlock machine, the napkin may be
   finished off with a narrow rolled hem in blue sewing
   thread.

Paisley tea cosy

Materials

Paisley cotton fabric: 30 cm × 60 cm
Wadding or thin foam rubber: 30 cm × 60 cm
Lining: 30 cm × 60 cm
Blue and burgundy sewing thread
Burgundy bias binding: 62 cm
Tracing paper

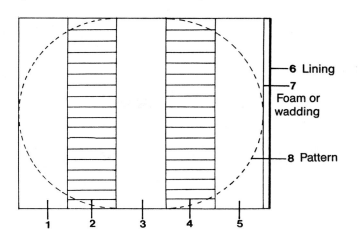

Sketch 13

Method

○ Trace Pattern 10 on p. 63 onto paper and cut out. Fold
   the cotton fabric in two pieces of 30 cm square. Place
   the pattern on the folded fabric and cut out two fabric
   pieces.
○ Use the same pattern to cut two pieces each from the
   wadding or foam and the lining.
○ Join the layers for the front together as follows: With
   right sides facing outward, place the paisley fabric
   and lining together with the thin foam in between.
○ Use straight stitch to work rows 3 cm apart through
   all three layers. Start in the centre of the tea cosy and
   work towards the sides.
○ Finish off the raw edges of all three layers together.
○ Repeat for the back of the tea cosy.
○ With right sides facing, place the front and back
   together and stitch a seam all the way round.
○ Turn to the right side and press the seam flat.
○ Finish off the bottom edge of the tea cosy with bur-
   gundy bias binding.
○ Join the ends of the bias binding and neaten all
   threads.

Paisley teapot stand

Materials

Paisley fabric: 29 cm square
Foam rubber or wadding: 29 cm square
Lining: 29 cm square
Blue and burgundy sewing thread
Burgundy bias binding: 90 cm
Tracing paper

Method

○ Draw a circle with a diameter of 27 cm onto the tracing paper.
○ Cut out the pattern and place it on the paisley fabric.

Pin in position and cut out the fabric according to the pattern.

○ Repeat with the foam/wadding and the lining.
○ With right sides facing outward, place the paisley fabric and lining together and place the foam/wadding in between. Pin and tack.
○ Use straight stitch to work rows 3 cm apart across both the length and breadth to form 3 cm squares (Sketch 14).
○ Finish off the raw edges of all three layers together.
○ Use the bias binding to finish off the outer edge of the teapot stand.
○ Join the ends of the bias binding and neaten all threads.
○ Press the teapot stand.

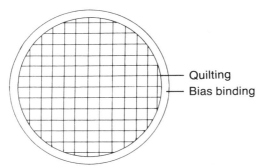

Quilting
Bias binding

Sketch 14

Burgundy pot-holder

Materials

Burgundy cotton fabric for front and back: 45 cm × 22 cm
Foam rubber or wadding: 22 cm square
Blue bias binding: 75 cm
Burgundy bias binding or satin ribbon for loop: 6 cm
Blue and burgundy sewing thread
Tracing paper

Method

○ Trace Pattern 11 on p. 64.
○ Cut 2 pieces from the burgundy fabric and 1 from the thin foam rubber or wadding.
○ With right sides facing outward, place the two burgundy sections together with the foam/wadding in between and pin the three layers together.
○ Use straight stitch to form neat blocks by stitching along the lines indicated.
○ Finish off the raw edges of all three layers together.
○ Finish off the outer edge of the pot-holder with blue bias binding. Join the ends of the bias binding and neaten all loose threads.
○ If bias binding is used for the loop, first fold it in half lengthways and stitch.

○ Fold the loop in half and stitch it into one corner of the pot-holder.
○ Press the pot-holder.

Striped place mats

Materials

For each place mat:
Pink-and-cream striped cotton fabric: 2 pieces, each 44 cm × 36 cm
Wadding or thin foam rubber: 44 cm × 36 cm
Lining: 44 cm × 36 cm
6 mm wide cream cotton anglaise lace: 3,4 m
Pink and cream sewing thread
Tracing paper

Method

○ Draw the place mat onto the tracing paper (44 cm × 36 cm) and cut out the pattern. The corners of the place mat are rounded (Sketch 15, point 1).
○ Cut 2 pieces from the striped fabric and 1 each from the lining and thin foam or wadding.
○ With right sides facing outward, place one piece of striped fabric and the lining together with the foam or wadding in between.
○ Pin the three layers together and use a double action straight stitch to stitch along the stripes of the front (Sketch 15, point 2).
○ Finish off the raw edges of all three layers together.
○ Join the ends of the lace neatly with a narrow French seam.
○ Gather the lace to fit around the place mat.
○ With right sides facing, place the lace on the striped fabric and stitch around the edge of the place mat (Sketch 15, point 3).

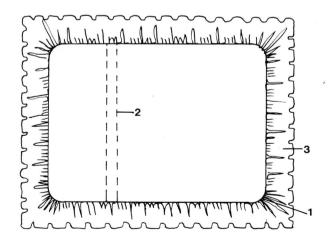

Sketch 15

25

- With right sides facing, place the second piece of striped fabric on the front with the frill in between the two layers. Make sure that the frill is folded to the inside.
- Stitch right around, but leave an opening of about 15 cm for turning the place mat to the right side.
- Neatly fold in the seam allowance at the opening and sew by hand.
- Press the place mat.

Pink tablecloth and napkins

To make a matching pink tablecloth for your dining-room table, measure the table and add about 20 cm all around. The overhang should be just the right length after the raw edges have been finished off with a rolled or 1 cm hem.

Materials

For each napkin:
Pink cotton fabric: 38 cm square
Cream machine embroidery thread

Method

- Cut the napkin according to the measurements given above.
- Finish off the raw edges with a row of cream satin stitches or a rolled hem.
- Press the napkin and fold.

Striped tea cosy

Materials

Pink-and-cream striped cotton fabric: 2 pieces, each 40 cm (width) × 28 cm (height)
Thin foam rubber or wadding: 2 pieces, each 40 cm × 28 cm
Lining: 2 pieces, each 40 cm × 28 cm
Pink fabric for frill: 142 cm × 10 cm
Pink and cream sewing thread
Pink bias binding: 58 cm
Tissue paper
Tracing paper

Method

- Trace Pattern 12 on p. 65 onto tracing paper and cut out.
- Use to cut 2 pieces each from striped fabric, lining and thin foam or wadding.
- Place the fabric front, right side up, on the foam or wadding front and pin both in place on the tissue paper. Using straight stitch, stitch along the outer edges of the wide pink stripes through all three layers. Remove the tissue paper once the stitching has been completed.

- With right sides facing outward, place the quilted front on the lining and finish off the raw edges together.
- Assemble the three layers of the back in the same way and finish off the raw edges.
- With right sides facing, fold the strip for the frill in half lengthways.
- Stitch the two short sides.
- Turn the frill to the right side, press the seams and iron the fold flat.
- Gather the frill strip to fit between the two points indicated.
- With right sides facing, stitch the frill to the front.
- Place the back and the front together with right sides facing and the frill in between.
- Stitch the seam around the curve and press neatly.
- Finish off the bottom edge of the tea cosy with pink bias binding.
- Join the ends of the bias binding and neaten all threads.
- Press the tea cosy.

Striped pot-holder

Materials

Pink-and-cream striped cotton fabric: 2 pieces, each 20 cm square
Thin foam rubber or wadding: 2 pieces, each 20 cm square
Lining: 20 cm square
6 mm wide cream satin ribbon for loop: 6 cm
Pink or cream bias binding: 85 cm
Pink sewing thread
Tracing paper

Method

- Trace Pattern 13 on p. 66 onto tracing paper and cut out.
- Cut two pieces from the striped fabric and one each from the lining and thin foam or wadding.
- Place the lining underneath, the foam or wadding in between and one piece of the striped fabric on top, right side up.
- Use double action straight stitch to stitch through all three layers along the outer edges of the pink stripes.
- Place the second piece of striped fabric under the lining with the right side facing outward.
- Finish off the raw edges of all the layers together.
- Fold the satin ribbon in half and place it in one corner as shown in Sketch 16.
- Finish off the outer edge of the pot-holder with the bias binding.
- Join the ends of the bias binding and press the pot-holder.

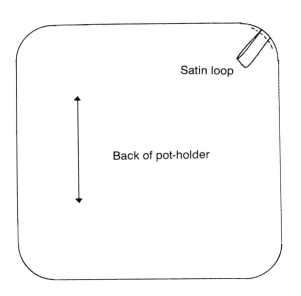

Satin loop

Back of pot-holder

Sketch 16

Cushion with parrot appliqué

A beautiful handpainted pot served as inspiration for this cushion cover. Give your imagination free rein and play around with colours and textures to make your own cushion.

Materials

Purple cotton fabric for front: 40 cm square
Purple cotton fabric for back: 40 cm × 60 cm
Remnants in different colours for appliqué
Lead-grey machine embroidery thread
Purple sewing thread
1 wobbly eye with a diameter of about 16 mm
Tissue paper
Glue stick
Tracing paper

Method

○ Trace Pattern 14a and 14b on pp. 67 and 68 and carefully cut out each piece.
○ Cut the pieces from the remnants. Make sure that the grain of the fabric of each pattern piece runs in the correct direction to prevent the appliqué puckering.
○ With right side facing up, place the fabric for the front of the cushion onto a piece of tissue paper. Carefully place the cut sections of the parrot next to each other on the fabric to form the design.
○ Glue the fabric pieces lightly onto the base fabric.
○ Tack all the pieces in place. Make sure that there are no spaces between the different sections of the motif.
○ Using the lead-grey machine embroidery thread, stitch all the pieces in place with a row of dense satin stitches. Keep the tissue paper under the fabric while stitching to prevent the stitches pulling. Neaten all threads.

○ Divide the fabric for the back of the cushion into two equal sections, each 40 cm × 30 cm. Finish off one 40 cm raw edge on each section. Fold over a 1 cm hem along these edges and stitch.
○ Place one back section on the front with right sides facing, and the hem in the centre. Stitch around the raw edges. Repeat with the second back section.
○ Finish off all four raw edges, turn to the right side and press.
○ Sew the eye in position and place a cushion in the cover.
○ Remember to be careful when ironing the cushion cover. If you touch the plastic eye with the iron, the heat will melt it.

Stylish bathrooms

The bathroom need not be the most neglected room in the house.
Add a little style to your bathroom by decorating it
in colours that tastefully complement each other.
Frame an embroidered picture for the wall and cover the tissue
box to match your make-up bag. Ordinary towels become
something special with the addition of
attractive decorative borders.

Embroidered picture

Materials

For the two embroidered pictures:
Linen or cotton to embroider
DMC stranded embroidery cotton: 1 skein each 758,
    948, 334, 522 and 543
Embroidery diagram
Embroidery needle
Embroidery frame
Tracing paper

Method

○ Transfer the embroidery diagram (Pattern 15a or 15b
    on pp. 68 and 69) onto the fabric.
○ Place the fabric in the embroidery frame.
○ Complete the embroidery according to the diagram.
    Use satin stitch for the flowers and leaves, stem stitch
    for the scrolls and colonial knots for the flower
    centres. The lines on the diagram indicate the direc-
    tion of the stitches.
○ Neaten all loose threads and press lightly on the
    wrong side.
○ Have the embroidery mounted and framed.

Decorative toilet soap sachet

Materials

Small-patterned cotton fabric: 37 cm × 16 cm
3 cm wide matching lace: 32 cm
16 mm wide apricot satin ribbon: 40 cm
Sewing thread
Elastic band, two satin leaves and a satin rose or other
    flower

Method

○ Neatly finish off the two short sides of the fabric.
○ Stitch the lace along the two finished edges (Sketch
    17, point 1).
○ With right sides facing, fold the fabric in half.
○ Stitch the two side seams (Sketch 17, point 2). Make
    sure that the seams are very neat at the opening of the
    bag.
○ Finish off the raw edges of the two seams and neaten
    all loose threads.
○ Turn the bag to the right side and press.
○ Place a bar of soap in the bag and close the opening
    with the elastic band.
○ Insert the two leaves and the flower into the elastic
    band.
○ Tie the satin ribbon over the elastic band.

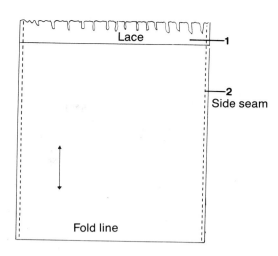

Sketch 17

Table centre

Materials

Cotton fabric: 26 cm square
3 cm wide blue cotton lace: 1,3 m
Apricot machine embroidery thread

Method

○ Cut out a circle with a diameter of 24 cm from the cot-
    ton fabric.
○ Finish off the raw edge all round.
○ Join the ends of the lace and gather to fit around the
    fabric circle. Pin in place and space gathers evenly.
○ Zigzag the lace onto the edge of the fabric.
○ Using the apricot machine embroidery thread, work
    a row of dense satin stitches over the zigzag.
○ Press the table centre.

Guest towel with embroidered border

Materials

Apricot guest towel: 55 cm × 32 cm
Cream cotton fabric for embroidery: 13 cm × 34 cm
DMC stranded embroidery cotton: 1 skein each 334,
    758, 948, 543 and 522
16 mm wide apricot satin ribbon: 34 cm
8 mm wide blue satin ribbon: 34 cm
5 cm wide cream cotton anglaise lace: 34 cm
Blue and apricot sewing thread
Embroidery frame
Embroidery needle
Tracing paper

Method

○ Transfer the embroidery diagram (Pattern 16 on p. 69) onto the cream fabric.
○ Place the fabric in the embroidery frame.
○ Complete the embroidery according to the diagram. Use satin stitch for the flowers and leaves, stem stitch for the scrolls and colonial knots for the flower centres. The lines on the diagram indicate the direction of the stitches.
○ Neaten all loose threads and press lightly on the wrong side.
○ Fold over a 1 cm hem on the short sides of the fabric.
○ Pin the embroidered strip 5 cm from the fringed edge of the towel (Sketch 18, point 1).
○ Using straight stitch, stitch the sides of the fabric onto the towel (Sketch 18, point 2). Zigzag the two long edges.
○ Fold in 1 cm at both ends of the apricot satin ribbon and stitch it onto the lower edge of the embroidery (Sketch 18, point 3).
○ Fold in 1 cm at both ends of the cream lace and stitch it onto the upper edge of the embroidery. The scalloped edge must point upwards (Sketch 18, point 4).
○ Fold in 1 cm at both ends of the blue satin ribbon and, using criss-cross stitches, stitch it over the row of stitches on the cream lace (Sketch 18, point 5).
○ Neaten all loose threads and press very lightly.

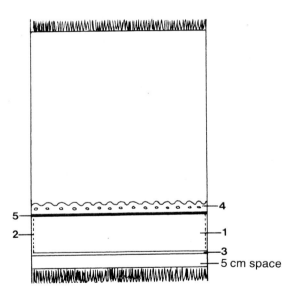

Sketch 18

Guest towel with fabric border

Materials

Blue guest towel: 55 cm × 32 cm
Patterned cotton fabric: 10 cm × 34 cm
16 mm wide apricot satin ribbon: 34 cm
Apricot machine embroidery thread

Method

○ Finish off the long raw edges of the fabric strip. Fold over a 1 cm hem at each short end.
○ Stitch the strip onto the towel 6 cm from the fringed edge. Use zigzag for the long edges and straight stitch for the sides.
○ Use the apricot machine embroidery thread to work a row of dense satin stitches along the lower edge of the fabric strip.
○ Fold in 1 cm at both ends of the satin ribbon and stitch it onto the upper edge of the fabric strip.
○ Neaten all loose threads and press the fabric strip very lightly.

Bath towel with rose appliqué

Materials

Cream towel: 69 cm × 129 cm
7 cm wide decorative border with rose motif: 72 cm
1,5 cm wide pointed cotton lace: 145 cm
6 mm wide apricot satin ribbon: 145 cm
Matching rose motif from floral cotton fabric
Cream and apricot sewing thread
Cream machine embroidery thread

Method

○ Tack the rose motif onto the right side of the towel. Place it in the centre, about 15 cm from the one edge.
○ Place tissue paper under the towel before stitching to prevent the motif puckering and to keep the stitches even. Using cream machine embroidery thread, stitch around the motif with a row of dense satin stitches. Make sure that the stitches are not too narrow, otherwise the fabric will fray when the towel is washed.
○ Fold over a 1,5 cm hem at both ends of the decorative border and zigzag it onto the towel below the appliquéd motif, about 5 cm from the edge.
○ Divide the cotton lace into two equal lengths. Fold in the raw edges until each piece fits exactly onto the towel and, with the points facing outwards, stitch with a narrow zigzag onto the edges of the decorative border.
○ Divide the apricot satin ribbon into two equal lengths and, using criss-cross stitch, stitch it onto the edge of the lace.
○ Press the appliqué lightly on the wrong side.

Face towel with decorative border

Materials

Apricot face towel: 49 cm × 99 cm
9 cm wide cream cotton lace: 52 cm
8 cm wide decorative border with rose motif: 52 cm
8 mm wide cream satin ribbon: 104 cm
Cream sewing thread

Method

○ Fold in the raw edges of the cotton lace until it fits exactly onto the towel.
○ Place the lace on the edge of the towel with the scalloped edge pointing outwards and stitch right around.
○ Place the decorative border next to the lace. Fold in the two raw edges and, using straight stitch, stitch right around the decorative border.
○ Divide the satin ribbon into two equal lengths, fold in the raw edges and stitch, using criss-cross stitch, onto both edges of the decorative border.
○ Neaten all the loose threads and press.

Hint: Any towel can be decorated in this way. Determine how much lace, ribbon or fabric you will need by measuring the width of the towel and adding at least 1 cm at each end for the folding in of the raw edges.

Always wash all fabrics to be used for trimming before cutting and stitching. It is essential that all trimmings must be washable and that all loose threads are neatened to prevent the stitches coming undone in the wash.

Cushion with embroidered rose motif

Materials

Cream cotton fabric for the front: 40 cm square
Cream cotton fabric for the back: 40 cm × 60 cm
Cream fabric to embroider: 18 cm square
25 mm wide cream satin ribbon: 1,6 m
16 mm wide apricot satin ribbon: 1,6 m
6 mm wide bright apricot satin ribbon: 1,6 m
DMC stranded embroidery cotton: 1 skein each 225, 224, 353, 223, 524 and 320
8 cm wide cream cotton lace: 3 m
Apricot and cream sewing thread
Embroidery frame
Embroidery needle
Tracing paper

Method

○ Transfer the embroidery diagram (Pattern 17 on p. 70) onto the fabric. Finish off the raw edges on the fabric.
○ Place the fabric in the embroidery frame and complete the embroidery according to the diagram. Use satin stitch for the rose petals and leaves and stem stitch for the stalks. The lines on the diagram indicate the direction of the stitches.
○ Press the embroidery on the wrong side and place it, right side up, on the right side of the front of the cushion cover.
○ Pin the motif exactly in the centre of the front. Tack and then stitch the embroidered piece in position.
○ Divide all three satin ribbons into 40 cm lengths.
○ Place the wide apricot satin ribbon on the two side edges of the embroidered panel (Sketch 19, point 1). Stitch the ribbon neatly in place.
○ Stitch the other two wide apricot satin ribbons onto the upper and lower edges of the embroidered panel (Sketch 19, point 2).
○ Place the cream satin ribbon directly against the apricot ribbon on either side of the embroidery (Sketch 19, point 3).
○ Neatly stitch the two lengths of ribbon.
○ Place the remaining two lengths of cream ribbon above and below the embroidery, directly against the apricot ribbon (Sketch 19, point 4).
○ Stitch neatly in place.
○ Leave a 2 cm space and stitch the narrow apricot satin ribbon in place using criss-cross stitch (Sketch 19, point 5). As previously done, first stitch the ribbons at the sides and then the remaining two at the top and bottom.
○ Join the two ends of the cream lace and gather evenly until it fits around the front of the cover.
○ With right sides facing, stitch the lace to the front. Allow enough fullness at the corners to prevent the lace pulling.
○ Divide the back of the cover into two equal parts, each 40 cm × 30 cm. Finish off one 40 cm raw edge on

both sections. Fold over a 1 cm hem along these edges and stitch.

- Place one back section on the front with right sides facing and the hem in the centre. Stitch around the raw edges. Repeat with the other back section.
- Finish off the four raw edges, neaten all loose threads and turn the cover to the right side.
- Press the seams lightly and place a cushion inside the cover.

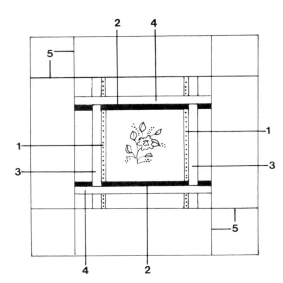

Sketch 19

Toilet soap sachet

Materials

1 bar of scented toilet soap
Floral (or any patterned) cotton fabric: 24 cm square
Matching lace – any width from 2-4 cm: 135 cm
Elastic band
14 mm wide satin ribbon: 45 cm
3 silk rose leaves
1 silk rose

Method

- Cut a circle with a diameter of 22 cm from the fabric.
- Finish off the raw edges.
- Join the two ends of the lace and gather until it fits around the fabric circle. Stitch the lace onto the fabric using criss-cross stitch.
- Place the fabric, wrong side up, on the work surface.
- Place the soap in the middle of the fabric.
- Pull the fabric circle tightly around the soap and tie it with the elastic band.
- Carefully insert the three leaves and the rose into the elastic.
- Tie the satin ribbon over the elastic and make a pretty bow near the rose and its leaves.

Tissue box cover

Materials

Floral cotton fabric for the centre strip: 2 pieces, each 49 cm × 7,5 cm
Floral cotton fabric for the side panels: 2 pieces, each 26 cm × 11,5 cm
Matching plain fabric for frills: 6 cm × 1,6 m
Thin foam rubber: 2 pieces, each 49 cm × 7,5 cm, and 2 pieces, each 26 cm × 11,5 cm
Lining: 2 pieces, each 49 cm × 7,5 cm, and 2 pieces, each 26 cm × 11,5 cm
6 mm wide green satin ribbon: 60 cm
Matching bias binding for piping: 90 cm
Cream sewing thread

Method

- Cut two centre strips and two side panels from each of the floral cotton fabric, lining and foam according to the measurements given above.
- Cut the frill from the plain fabric according to the measurements given above.
- Assemble the three layers of the centre strips and side panels as follows: the lining and floral fabric with wrong sides facing and the thin foam in between.
- Finish off the raw edges of each pattern piece together.
- Mark the middle point of each of the centre strips (Sketch 20a, point 1). Also mark the points 9 cm on either side of the middle point.
- With right sides facing, place the two centre strips together and make sure the marks on both match.
- Stitch the two centre strips together (Sketch 20b, point 2), but leave an opening of 18 cm in the middle between the points indicated (Sketch 20b, point 3).
- Open up the seam and topstitch both sides with double action straight stitch 2 cm from the seam (Sketch 20b, point 4).
- Divide the strip for the frill into two equal lengths. With wrong sides facing, fold them in half lengthways and stitch the short sides of each frill. Turn to the right side and iron the fold flat.
- Gather both frill strips and stitch one to each of the two long edges of the centre strip. However, start and finish 2 cm from the ends (Sketch 20b, point 5). This leaves enough space for finishing off the bottom edge of the cover.
- Pin the two side panels to the centre strip, making sure that they are exactly opposite each other.
- Stitch the side panels to the centre strip. Clip the centre strip on either side of the corners so that the fabric will fit neatly over the corners.
- Use bias binding to finish off the bottom edge of the cover.
- Divide the satin ribbon into two equal lengths and tie each into a bow.
- Sew a bow onto each side of the opening (Sketch 20b, point 6).

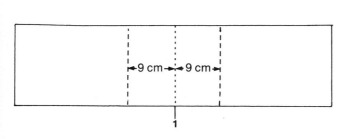

←9 cm→←9 cm→

1

Sketch 20a

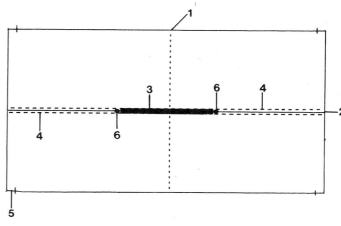

Sketch 20b

Make-up bag

Materials

Floral cotton fabric: 30 cm × 60 cm
Thin foam rubber: 30 cm × 60 cm
Plastic lining: 30 cm × 60 cm
Pink cotton fabric for foldover flap: 15 cm × 12 cm
8 mm wide green satin ribbon: 50 cm
Pink bias binding: 45 cm
Velcro: 2 cm × 1 cm
4 cm wide cream cotton lace: 12 cm
Matching sewing thread
Tissue paper
Tracing paper

Method

- Trace Patterns 18a, 18b and 18c on p. 71 and 72.
- Cut the front, back and gusset from the floral fabric, the foam and the lining. Cut the foldover flap from the pink fabric, the foam and the lining.
- Cut a frill strip of 60 cm × 9 cm from the floral fabric. With wrong sides facing, fold it in half lengthways, iron the fold flat and gather until it measures 40 cm.
- Place the pink foldover flap with the right side up on the matching piece of foam. Place a layer of tissue paper underneath and decorate as follows.
- Stitch a strip of lace in the centre of the pink fabric (Sketch 21, point 2).
- Stitch some of the green satin ribbon over these stitches and two more pieces 1,5 cm on either side of the lace (Sketch 21, point 2 and 3).
- With right sides facing, stitch the gathered frill around the rounded edge of the flap (Sketch 21, point 4).
- Place the lining on the right side of the flap. Stitch a 5 mm seam around the rounded edge and turn to the right side.

- Stitch half the Velcro to the centre of the lining, 1 cm from the lower edge.
- Assemble the three layers for each of the front, back and gusset and finish off all the edges.
- With right sides facing, stitch the gusset to the rounded edge of the front.
- Stitch the remaining Velcro to the centre of the right side of the front, 5 cm from the lower edge.
- With right sides facing, stitch the back to the other edge of the gusset. Turn the bag to the right side.
- With right sides facing, place the flap on the back and stitch 5 mm from the edge.
- Use bias binding to finish off the remaining raw edge on the front and gusset.
- Sew a small green satin bow to the flap.

> **Hint:** Bear in mind that the articles described above make attractive gifts. So next time, rather than rushing out to buy a present, make something yourself.

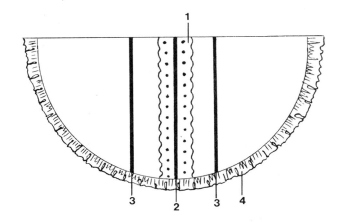

Sketch 21

Toddler's delight

*Choose a cheerful theme for your little one's room. Here chubby
bears romp on a holdall and cushion. Cheeky clowns in
bright eye-catching colours parade against the wall
and on a towel and playpen blanket. For your little girl's
favourite doll there is a pillow and blanket. Adapt
these ideas to your own colour scheme and bear
them in mind as clever gifts.*

Holdall with bear motif

Materials

Cotton fabric with motif for front: 34 cm square
Matching cotton fabric for back: 34 cm square
Lining: 2 pieces, each 34 cm square
Thin foam rubber: 2 pieces, each 34 cm square
Matching cotton fabric for gusset: 105 cm × 12 cm
Thin foam rubber for gusset: 105 cm × 12 cm
Lining for gusset: 105 cm × 12 cm
Matching fabric for handles: 2 strips, each 32 cm × 9 cm
White bias binding: 1,64 m
Matching sewing thread
Tracing paper

Method

○ Cut out all pattern pieces according to the measurements given above.
○ Assemble the three layers for each of the front, back and gusset as follows: The lining and cotton fabric with wrong sides facing and the foam in between.
○ Finish off the raw edges of the three layers together.
○ Work two rows of straight stitches around the edge of the front as shown in Sketch 22a. Work equally spaced rows of straight stitches over the length of the back and the gusset as shown in Sketch 22b and 22c.
○ With right sides facing, stitch the gusset to the front. Starting at the top of one side, stitch the side, the base and then the second side. Clip the gusset about 3 cm on either side of each corner so that the fabric fits smoothly and to prevent the gusset puckering.
○ The gusset will be slightly longer than the front. Trim away the excess fabric on one end.
○ Stitch the back to the other side of the gusset. Make sure that the front and back match perfectly, otherwise the bag will be crooked.
○ Finish off the top edge of the bag with bias binding.
○ Fold the two strips for the handles in half lengthways with right sides facing. Stitch all the way round, but leave an opening for turning. Turn to the right side, sew up the opening by hand and press.
○ Decorate the handles by stitching white bias binding along the centre.
○ Stitch the two ends of one handle to the top edge of the front, each 7,5 cm from a corner. Attach the other handle to the back in the same way. Work two rows of stitches diagonally across each end of the handles as shown in Sketch 22d. This will secure the handles even if the bag gets rather heavy.
○ Press the seams and enjoy your handiwork.

Hint: Decorate a towel with a strip of fabric showing a bear or other suitable motif. Finish it off with lace, a decorative stitch and satin ribbon in a contrasting colour. Follow the instructions for all the decorated towels described previously.

Co-ordinate an ordinary covered clothes hanger into the scheme by adding a small piece of lace and a large button with a bear motif.

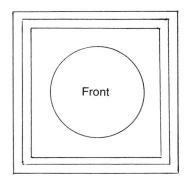

Sketch 22a

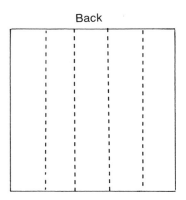

Sketch 22b

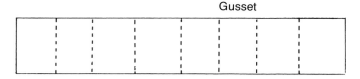

Sketch 22c

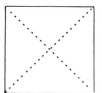

Sketch 22d

Cushion with bear motif

Materials

Patterned blue cotton fabric for the front: 36 cm × 35 cm
Patterned blue cotton fabric for the back: 36 cm × 56 cm
Fabric with motif large enough for the oval shape
6 cm wide white cotton lace: 4,6 cm
37 mm wide white satin ribbon: 75 cm
6 mm wide red satin ribbon: 85 cm
Red machine embroidery thread
Blue sewing thread
Tracing paper

Method

○ Trace the oval shape for the front of the cushion according to Pattern 19 on p. 73.
○ Place it on the fabric with the motif (the motif must be exactly in the centre) and cut out.
○ Finish off the raw edge of the oval.
○ Pin the motif to the centre of the cushion front, with both right sides up. Tack in position and stitch (Sketch 23, point 1).
○ Measure 1,75 of the white lace, join the ends and gather to fit around the oval motif. Use criss-cross stitch to stitch the lace around the motif (Sketch 23, point 2).
○ Using criss-cross stitch, stitch the red satin ribbon on top of this row of stitches (Sketch 23, point 3). Fold the ends of the ribbon to the wrong side before stitching to prevent it fraying.
○ Stitch a row of decorative stitches with red machine embroidery thread around the oval, 1 cm inside the red satin ribbon (Sketch 23, point 4).
○ Tie the white satin ribbon into a bow and sew the bow onto the red satin ribbon (Sketch 23, point 5).
○ Join the ends of the remaining lace and gather until it fits around the outer edge of the front. With right sides facing, stitch the lace around the front (Sketch 23, point 6).
○ Divide the back of the cover into two equal parts, each 36 cm × 27,5 cm. Finish off one of the 36 cm raw edges on both parts. Fold over a 1 cm hem along these edges and stitch.
○ Place one back section on the front with right sides facing the lace in between and the hem in the centre. Stitch along the raw edges. Repeat with the other back section.
○ Finish off the four raw edges and turn the cover to the right side.
○ Press the seams lightly and place a cushion inside the cover.

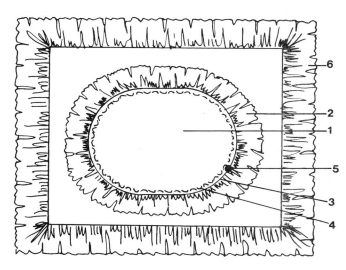

Sketch 23

Playpen blanket with clown appliqué

Materials

Plain yellow fabric for the front: 48 cm × 64 cm
Patterned strip for the front: 12 cm × 2,7 m
Plain yellow fabric for the back: 72 cm × 86 cm
Thick wadding: 72 cm × 86 cm
Fairly large pieces of fabric in suitable colours for the appliqué
Red, yellow, green, blue, white and black machine embroidery thread
Yellow sewing thread
Tissue paper
Glue stick
Small bell
Tracing paper

Method

○ Trace Pattern 20 on pp. 74-75. Enlarge the clown 100% so that it is 50 cm long.
○ Neatly cut out the pattern pieces for the clown and pin them to the different fabrics.
○ Cut out the fabric.
○ Place a layer of tissue paper under the plain yellow front. Carefully pin all the pieces for the clown to the base fabric. When you are sure there are no gaps between the different pieces, glue each piece lightly in position with the glue stick.
○ Use straight stitch to stitch 2 mm inside the edge of each piece and then use the machine embroidery thread and a row of dense satin stitches to stitch all the pieces in position.
○ Remove the tissue paper from the back and lightly press the appliqué. Sew the bell in position.
○ Divide the long strip of patterned fabric for the outer edge into two 48 cm lengths and two 87 cm lengths.
○ With right sides facing, stitch the two 48 cm lengths to the top and bottom edges of the plain fabric (Sketch

24, points 1 and 2). Press the seams open and then stitch the two 87 cm strips to the two sides of the plain fabric in the same way (Sketch 25, points 3 and 4). Press these seams open too.

○ Place the wadding under the front and tack the two layers together. Place a layer of tissue paper under the wadding and stitch along the edge of the patterned fabric, as closely as possible to the seam (Sketch 24, point 5). With yellow sewing thread, stitch a row of straight stitches along the edge of the yellow fabric, as closely as possible to the seam (Sketch 24, point 6).

○ Stitch two more rows of stitches on the yellow fabric, each 1 cm inside the previous row (Sketch 24, points 7 and 8).

○ With red machine embroidery thread, work a row of decorative stitches on the yellow fabric, 4 cm from the edge (Sketch 24, point 9). The front is now completed.

○ With right sides facing, pin the front to the back and tack along the outer edge.

○ Stitch all the way round, leaving a 20 cm opening for turning. Finish off the raw edges of the seams and turn the blanket to the right side.

○ Fold the seam allowance at the opening to the inside and sew the opening closed by hand.

○ Press the side seams and then work a double action straight stitch 1 cm from the outer edge (Sketch 24, point 10). Neatly work away the loose threads.

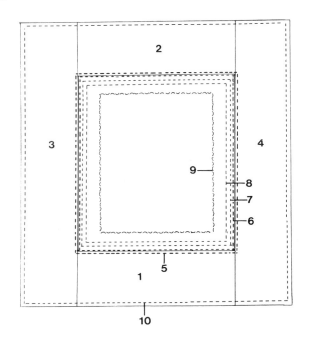

Sketch 24

Cushion cover with strip patchwork

Materials

Remnants of the previous blanket, joined in strips for the front: 40 cm × 28 cm
Matching fabric for the back: 60 cm × 28 cm
Patterned fabric for frill: 7 cm × 2,3 m
1 cm wide red cotton lace: 2,3 m
Red sewing thread

Method

○ Stitch about four strips of fabric together. Press all the seams open and then cut a front of 40 cm × 28 cm from the patchwork. Make sure that the strips for the front are straight.

○ Finish off one raw edge of the frill and stitch the red lace onto the finished edge.

○ Join the ends of the frill and gather to fit around the front.

○ With right sides facing, stitch the frill to the front.

○ Divide the back into two equal parts, each 30 cm × 28 cm. Finish off one 28 cm raw edge on each section.

Fold over a 1 cm hem along these edges and stitch.
- Place one back section on the front with right sides facing, the frill in between and the hem in the centre. Stitch along the raw edges. Repeat with the other back section.
- Finish off the four raw edges, neaten all loose threads and turn the cover to the right side.
- Press the seams lightly and place a baby pillow inside the cover.

Towel with clown appliqué

Materials

Red towel: 69 cm × 129 cm
Remnants in different colours for the appliqué motif
Green, yellow, black and red machine embroidery thread
Tissue paper
Large round blue button
Tracing paper

Method

- Trace the clown's head from Pattern 20 on p. 74 and enlarge it 100%.
- Neatly cut out the pattern pieces for the clown and pin them to the various fabrics.
- Cut out the fabric.
- Place a layer of tissue paper under the towel. Carefully pin all the pieces for the clown onto the towel. When you are sure there are no gaps between the various pieces, glue each piece lightly in position with the glue stick.
- Use straight stitch to stitch 2 mm inside the edge of each piece and then use the machine embroidery thread and a row of dense satin stitches to stitch all the pieces in position.
- Remove the tissue paper from the back and lightly press the appliqué. Sew the button in position.
- By way of a change, a frill has been sewn around the face of the clown on the towel in the photograph.

Framed cross-stitch clown

Materials

14-count Aïda cross-stitch fabric: about 20 cm × 30 cm
DMC stranded embroidery cotton: 2 skeins each 820 and 700; 1 skein each 823, 817, 310, 225, 741, 743, 996, white and ecru; scraps of 745, 817, 741, 743, 996, 820 and 700
Embroidery needle
Embroidery frame

Method

- Cut the cross-stitch fabric to the size of the picture plus a 4 cm border all around. In order to frame the picture properly, it is important to leave ample fabric around the edge.
- Zigzag the raw edges. If you do not have a sewing machine, use masking tape to prevent the edges from fraying.
- Determine the centre of the fabric as follows: Fold the fabric in half to find the centre of the side. Using ordinary machine thread, sew a tacking stitch over each cross-stitch sized square across the length of the material. Do the same with the width. The intersection of these two lines is the centre point. Start embroidering here and complete the design according to the embroidery diagram (Sketch 25) in cross-stitch and Holbein stitch.
- Press the completed article on the wrong side using a hot iron and a damp cloth.
- Have the completed picture framed. As it is very colourful, a wide variety of colours can be used for the mounts.

Size: 84 stitches wide
× 133 stitches high

	DMC-no.
/	823
A	820
B	817
■	310
w	white
o	225
v	ecru
E	700
N	741
R	743
●	996
K	scraps of 745, 817, 741, 743, 996, 820 and 700 are used to fill this area. However, it may also be worked in one colour only, if preferred. Outline all sections with one strand of black.

Sketch 25

Doll's set

Quilted blanket

Materials

Striped cotton fabric for the front: 40 cm × 48 cm
Matching plain fabric for the back: 40 cm × 48 cm
12 cm wide pink anglaise cotton lace: 3,2 m
Pink or any other matching sewing thread
Wadding: 40 cm × 48 cm
Tissue paper: 40 cm × 48 cm

Method

○ With right side up, place the striped cotton fabric on the wadding. Place the tissue paper under the wadding and pin all three layers together. The tissue paper will prevent the wadding catching on the machine.
○ Starting at the bottom, work rows of straight stitches 7 cm apart over the width of the fabric (Sketch 26, point 1). The last strip will be slightly narrower. Remove the tissue paper once the quilting is complete.
○ Finish off each end of the pink anglaise lace with a narrow hem. Gather the lace to fit around the edge of the blanket.
○ With right sides facing, stitch the lace to the front of the blanket. Start 1,5 cm from the top on the one side and end the same distance from the top on the other side (Sketch 26, point 2).
○ With right sides facing and the lace in between, place the plain fabric on the front. Stitch around the edge, leaving an opening of 15 cm for turning.
○ Turn the blanket to the right side, fold the seam allowance to the inside and sew the opening closed by hand.
○ Press the seams and the quilted area.

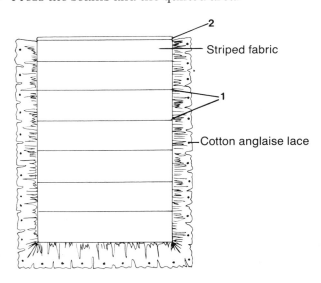

Sketch 26

Labels on sketch: 2, Striped fabric, 1, Cotton anglaise lace

Pillow case

Materials

Striped cotton fabric for the front: 31 cm × 24 cm
Matching plain fabric for the back: 51 cm × 24 cm
12 cm wide pink anglaise cotton lace: 2 m
Pink sewing thread

Method

○ Cut out all the pieces to the measurements given above.
○ Trim the raw edge of the anglaise lace by 3 cm to make it narrower.
○ Join the two ends of the lace and gather to fit around the edge of the pillow case. With right sides facing, stitch the lace to the front.
○ Divide the back into two equal parts, each 25,5 cm × 24 cm. Finish off one 24 cm raw edge on each section. Fold over a 1 cm hem along these edges and stitch.
○ Place one back section on the front with right sides facing, the lace in between and the hem in the centre. Stitch along the raw edges. Repeat with the other back section.
○ Finish off the four raw edges, neaten all loose threads and turn the cover to the right side.
○ Press the seams lightly and place a baby pillow inside the cover.

Pastels for the bedroom

Match the decor in your bedroom to an attractive bedspread and create a tranquil atmosphere with soft pastels. The pictures on the wall are embroidered in colour combinations that tone in with the rest of the room. Pastel shades are repeated in the lavishly decorated cushions, embroidered tablecloth and decorated straw hat.

Embroidered pictures

Materials

2 pieces thin white cotton or linen to embroider: each 20 cm square
Pink and purple seed pearls
DMC stranded embroidery cotton: 1 skein each 775, 745, 776, 340, 778, 211, 523 and 502
Embroidery needle
Embroidery frame
Tracing paper

Method

○ Transfer the embroidery diagram (Pattern 21 on p. 76) onto the fabric. Finish off the raw edges of the fabric.
○ Place the fabric in the embroidery frame and complete the embroidery. Use satin stitch for the flowers and small leaves and stem stitch for the large leaf and the stalks. The lines on the diagram indicate the direction of the stitches.
○ Neatly work away all the threads and press lightly on the wrong side.
○ Sew the seed pearls onto the picture as shown in the diagram. However, change this slightly for the second picture.
○ Have the embroidery mounted and framed. The choice of colours for the mounts is extremely important. Mounts complement the embroidery and enlarge the picture with the result that it becomes much more striking on a large wall.

Pink embroidered cushion

Materials

Thin white cotton to embroider: 17 cm × 19 cm
White cotton fabric for the front: 36 cm × 39 cm
White cotton fabric for the back: 36 cm × 59 cm
11 cm wide pink anglaise cotton lace: 5 m
8 mm wide purple satin ribbon: 95 cm
White and purple sewing thread
DMC stranded embroidery cotton: 1 skein each 775, 340, 523, 745, 211, 776, 778 and 502
Embroidery frame
Embroidery needle
Tracing paper

Method

○ Transfer the embroidery diagram (Pattern 21 on p. 76) onto the fabric. Omit the seed pearls on the cushion cover.
○ Place the fabric in the embroidery frame and complete the embroidery. Use satin stitch for the flowers and small leaves and stem stitch for the large leaf and the stalks. The lines on the embroidery diagram indicate the direction of the stitches.

○ Work away the loose threads and lightly press the embroidery on the wrong side.
○ Pin the embroidery to the centre of the front and tack in position.
○ Stitch the embroidery to the front (Sketch 27, point 1).
○ Stitch some of the wide pink anglaise lace, with the scalloped edge facing inward, around the embroidery. Fold the lace at the corners and strengthen with a straight stitch (Sketch 27, point 2).
○ Stitch the purple satin ribbon around the embroidery, 1 cm outside the scalloped edge of the pink lace (Sketch 27, point 3).
○ Join the ends of the remaining pink lace and gather to fit around the front (Sketch 27, point 4). With right sides facing, stitch the frill to the front. Trim the raw edges.
○ Divide the back of the cover into two equal parts, each 36 cm × 29,5 cm. Finish off one 36 cm raw edge on each part. Fold over a 1 cm hem along these edges and stitch.
○ Place one back section on the front with right sides facing, the lace in between and the hem in the centre. Stitch along the raw edges. Repeat with the other back section.
○ Finish off the four raw edges, neaten all loose threads and turn the cover to the right side.
○ Press the seams lightly and place a cushion inside the cover.

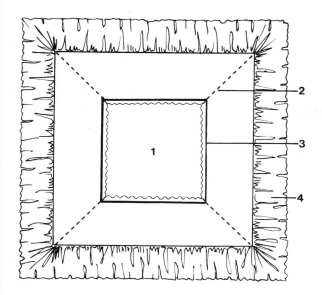

Sketch 27

Cushion with ribbon and lace trimmings

Materials

White cotton fabric for the front: 38 cm × 36 cm
White cotton fabric for the back: 38 cm × 56 cm
2 cm wide white insertion lace: 80 cm
4 cm wide pink insertion lace: 70 cm
11 cm wide pink anglaise cotton lace: 3 m
10 mm wide purple satin ribbon: 70 cm
10 mm wide pink satin ribbon: 75 cm
Purple machine embroidery thread
Pink and white sewing thread
2 pearl beads
Marking pen

Method

○ Fold the white front diagonally in half and place point A on point C (see Sketch 28). Mark the diagonal.
○ Using purple machine embroidery thread, work a row of decorative stitches along this line (Sketch 28, point 1).
○ Stitch some of the white insertion lace 1 cm away from the decorative stitches (Sketch 28, point 2).
○ Use criss-cross stitch to stitch pink satin ribbon 1 cm from the insertion lace (Sketch 28, point 3).
○ Use purple machine embroidery thread to work another row of decorative stitches 5 mm from the satin ribbon (Sketch 28, point 4).
○ Use criss-cross stitch to stitch purple satin ribbon 12 mm from the decorative stitches (Sketch 28, point 5).
○ Stitch some of the pink insertion lace 8 cm from the purple satin ribbon (Sketch 28, point 6).
○ Stitch a piece of pink satin ribbon onto one edge of the lace (Sketch 28, point 7).

○ Sew the two pearl beads where indicated (Sketch 28, point 8).
○ Now decorate the other half of the front. Leave an open space of 5,5 cm after the row of decorative stitches on the centre line and stitch the remaining pink insertion lace in place (Sketch 28, point 9).
○ Use criss-cross stitch to stitch pink satin ribbon 1,5 cm from the pink insertion lace (Sketch 28, point 10).
○ Work the next row of decorative stitches 5 mm from the satin ribbon and leave a 5 mm space between each of the following three rows. First work a row of decorative stitches in purple followed by purple satin ribbon and then another row of decorative stitches in purple (Sketch 28, points 11, 12 and 13).
○ Stitch the remaining white insertion lace 1,5 cm further on (Sketch 28, point 14).
○ Complete the decoration of the cushion front with another row of decorative stitches in purple, 5 mm from the insertion lace (Sketch 28, point 15).
○ Join the two ends of the pink anglaise lace. Gather the lace to fit around the cushion and, with right sides facing, stitch the frill to the front.
○ Divide the back of the cover into two equal parts, each 38 cm × 28 cm. Finish off one 38 cm raw edge on each part. Fold over a 1 cm hem along these edges and stitch.
○ Place one back section on the front with right sides facing, the lace in between and the hem in the centre. Stitch along the raw edges. Repeat with the second back section.
○ Finish off the four raw edges, neaten all loose threads and turn the cover to the right side.
○ Press the seams lightly and place a cushion inside the cover.

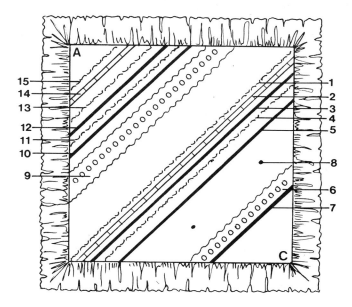

Sketch 28

45

Cream embroidered cushion

Materials

Cream fabric to embroider: 22 cm × 20 cm
Cream fabric for the front: 40 cm × 34 cm
Cream fabric for the back: 40 cm × 54 cm
DMC stranded embroidery cotton: 1 skein each 224, 225, 761, 754, 504, 368, 775, 746 and 3078
8 cm wide cream cotton lace: 4,5 m
25 mm wide apricot satin ribbon: 50 cm
Apricot machine embroidery thread
Cream sewing thread
Embroidery frame
Embroidery needle
Tracing paper

Method

○ Transfer the embroidery diagram (Pattern 22a on p. 76) onto the fabric.
○ Place the fabric in an embroidery frame and complete the embroidery. Use satin stitch for the flowers and leaves, stem stitch for the stalks and French knots for the blue flower clusters. The lines on the diagram indicate the direction of the stitches.
○ Work all loose threads away and lightly press the embroidery on the wrong side.
○ Trace the oval shape (Pattern 22b on p. 77). Place the pattern on the embroidered fabric so that the motif is exactly in the centre and cut it out.
○ Pin the embroidery to the centre of the cushion front and tack in position (Sketch 29a, point 1). Zigzag the two pieces together.
○ Measure 1,5 m of the cream lace, join the two ends and gather the lace to fit around the edge of the oval panel. Stitch in place using criss-cross stitch (Sketch 29a, point 2).
○ Work a row of decorative stitches in apricot, 1 cm inside the edge of the oval (Sketch 29a, point 3).
○ Tie the apricot satin ribbon into a bow and sew it in place where indicated (Sketch 29a, point 4).
○ Join the ends of the remaining lace and gather evenly to fit around the front.
○ With right sides facing, stitch the frill to the front (Sketch 29a, point 5).
○ Divide the back of the cover into two equal parts, each 40 cm × 27 cm. Finish off one 40 cm raw edge on each section. Fold over a 1 cm hem along these edges and stitch.
○ Place one back section on the front with right sides facing, the lace in between and the hem in the centre. Stitch along the raw edges (Sketch 29b). Repeat with the other back section.
○ Finish off the four raw edges, neaten all loose threads and turn the cover to the right side.
○ Press the seams lightly and place a cushion inside the cover.

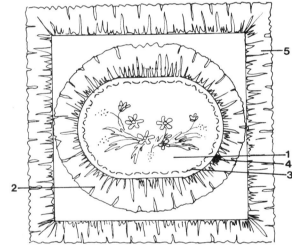

Sketch 29a

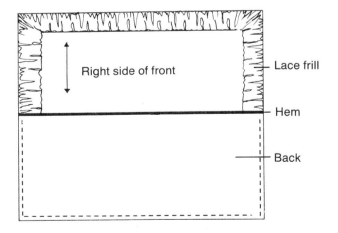

Sketch 29b

Blue-and-white embroidered cushion

Materials

Thin white cotton fabric to embroider: 20 cm square
White cotton fabric for the front: 40 cm square
White cotton fabric for the back: 40 cm × 60 cm
DMC stranded embroidery cotton: 1 skein each 3348,
  3363, 745, 312, 334 and 336
13 cm wide blue anglaise cotton lace: 4 m
4 cm wide white lace: 85 cm
25 mm wide blue satin ribbon: 50 cm
Blue and white sewing thread
Embroidery needle
Embroidery frame
Tracing paper

Method

○ Transfer the embroidery diagram (Pattern 23 on p.
  78) onto the fabric.
○ Place the fabric in the embroidery frame and complete the embroidery. Use stem stitch for the stalks
  and satin stitch for the flowers and leaves. The lines
  on the diagram indicate the direction of the stitches.
○ Work away all loose threads and lightly press the embroidery on the wrong side.
○ Cut the embroidery fabric in a circle with a diameter
  of 14 cm. The motif must be exactly in the centre.
○ Place the front of the cover, right side up, on the work
  surface (Sketch 30, point 1).
○ Pin the embroidered circle to the centre and zigzag in
  place (Sketch 30, point 2).
○ Measure 1,4 m of the blue lace. Join the two ends and
  gather the lace to fit around the edge of the circle.
  With right side up and using criss-cross stitch, stitch
  the lace around the edge of the circle (Sketch 30,
  point 3).
○ Join the two ends of the white lace and, forming small
  pleats, tack the lace around the circle. Use criss-cross
  stitch to stitch the lace on top of the previous stitches
  (Sketch 30, point 4).
○ Join the two ends of the remaining blue lace, gather
  and stitch the lace, using criss-cross stitch, 7 cm from
  the inner circle and underneath the first row of blue
  lace (Sketch 30, point 5).
○ Tie the blue satin ribbon into a bow and sew it where
  indicated (Sketch 30, point 6).
○ Divide the back of the cover into two equal parts, each
  40 cm × 30 cm. Finish off one 40 cm raw edge on
  each section. Fold over a 1 cm hem along these edges
  and stitch.
○ Place the one back section on the front with right
  sides facing and the hem in the centre. Stitch along
  the raw edges. Repeat with the other back section.
○ Finish off the four raw edges, neaten all loose threads
  and turn the cover to the right side.
○ Press the seams lightly and place a cushion inside
  the cover.

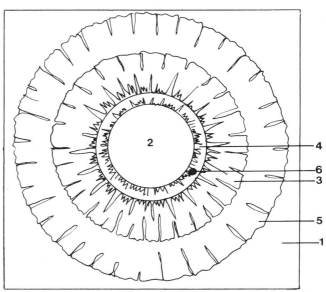

Sketch 30

White embroidered cushion

These two cushions (A and B) are made in the same way. However, each cushion has its own embroidery design and, in the case of cushion B, pearl beads are also sewn in amongst the flowers. As the round panel in the centre of cushion B is slightly smaller than that of cushion A, less lace is used.

Materials

White cotton fabric for the front: 35 cm square
White cotton fabric for the back: 35 × 55 cm
White cotton fabric to embroider: 22 cm square
6,5 cm wide white lace: 4,6 m for cushion A; 4,4 m for cushion B
DMC stranded embroidery cotton: For cushion A: 1 skein each 223, 3354, 225, 224, 502 and 504; For cushion B: 1 skein each 225, 224, 316, 369 and 368
23 small seed pearls (for cushion B only)
Pink machine embroidery thread
White sewing thread
Embroidery frame
Embroidery needle
Tracing paper

Method

○ Transfer the embroidery diagram (Pattern 24a on p. 78 for cushion A and Pattern 24b on p. 79 for cushion B) onto the fabric.
○ Place the fabric in an embroidery frame and complete the embroidery. Use satin stitch for all the leaves and flowers and stem stitch for the stalks. The lines on the diagram indicate the direction of the stitches.
○ Cut the embroidered fabric in a circle with a diameter of 20 cm for cushion A and 16 cm for cushion B.
○ Finish off the raw edge of the circle and press lightly on the wrong side.
○ Place the front of the cover, right side up, on the work surface (Sketch 31, point 1).
○ Pin the embroidered circle in the centre and zigzag around the edge (Sketch 31, point 2).
○ Measure 1,75 m of the white lace for cushion A or 1,55 m for cushion B. Join the two ends and, forming small pleats, tack the lace around the edge of the circle. With right side up, zigzag the lace in place (Sketch 31, point 3).
○ Using pink machine embroidery thread, work a row of decorative stitches 1 cm inside the edge of the embroidered circle (Sketch 31, point 4). Work a second row of decorative stitches on the front of the cushion, 1 cm from the outer edge of the lace frill (Sketch 31, point 5).
○ Join the ends of the remaining lace and gather to fit around the front. With right sides facing, stitch the lace to the front (Sketch 31, point 6).
○ Divide the back of the cover into two equal parts, each 35 cm × 27,5 cm. Finish off one 35 cm raw edge on each section. Fold over a 1 cm hem along these edges and stitch.

○ Place one section of the back on the front with right sides facing, the lace in between and the hem in the centre. Stitch along the raw edges. Repeat with the other back section.
○ Finish off the four raw edges, neaten all loose threads and turn the cover to the right side.
○ Press the seams lightly and place a cushion inside the cover.

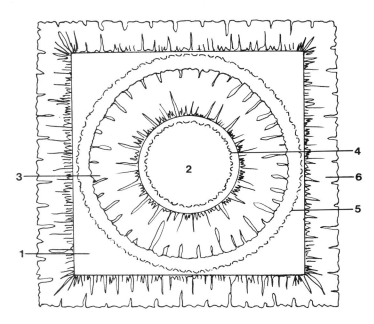

Sketch 31

48

Embroidered tablecloth

Materials

Cream fabric: 95 cm square
6 cm wide cream cotton lace: 4,9 m
DMC stranded embroidery cotton: 1 skein each 369, 3364, 794, 3041, 3042, 316, 778, 225, 3689, 224 and 746
Cream sewing thread
Embroidery needle
Embroidery frame
Tracing paper

Method

○ Transfer the embroidery diagram (Pattern 25 on p. 79) to one corner of the fabric.
○ Place the fabric in the embroidery frame and complete the embroidery according to the diagram. Use satin stitch for the flowers and leaves, stem stitch for the stalks and French knots for the clusters of blue flowers. The lines on the diagram indicate the direction of the stitches.
○ Work away all loose threads and lightly press the embroidery on the wrong side.
○ Stitch the cream cotton lace around the edge of the fabric and press the completed tablecloth.

Decorated straw hat

Materials

1 large straw hat
14 cm wide cream lace: 1,75 m
Cream cotton fabric to cover the crown of the hat: 40 cm × 60 cm
25 mm wide apricot satin ribbon: 2,6 m
16 mm wide apricot satin ribbon: 80 cm
15 dried rosebuds
Sprigs of dried gypsophila
Dried cream hydrangeas
12 small apricot silk roses
Cream crochet yarn
Thick, sharp-pointed needle
Cream sewing thread

Method

○ Tack rows 5 cm apart over the length of the cream fabric (i.e. seven 60 cm rows).
○ Gather all the tacking threads until the fabric measures 40 cm square. Make sure that the gathers are straight.
○ Place the gathered fabric over the crown of the hat. Pin the fabric to the hat in the front, at the back and at the sides.
○ Neatly pleat the fabric between the pins and use crochet yarn to sew it onto the hat. You can use a sewing machine to do this, or it can be sewn by hand. The crochet yarn is thick and will not easily pull through the straw.
○ Trim the excess fabric, 1 cm from the stitches.
○ Join the two ends of the cream lace. Gather the lace along one edge to fit around the crown of the hat. Sew the lace to the fabric all the way around the crown.
○ Measure 1,1 m of the broad satin ribbon, mark the centre and sew it to the back of the hat.
○ Sew the various flowers and remaining satin ribbons alternately in place around the crown so that they cover the stitches that hold the lace and fabric in place. Lastly, tie all the ribbons in bows. The number of bows can vary according to choice.
○ Remember that dried flowers break off very easily and will also fade in strong light. Silk flowers and leaves can also be used if dried materials are not available.

Christmas cheer

Here are a few ideas for Christmas decorations that, apart from the traditional Christmas tree, will add a festive atmosphere to your home. There is a welcoming Christmas wreath for the front door and the framed cross-stitch pictures, Christmas stockings and cute little Christmas mouse can also serve as gifts.

Framed cross-stitch pictures

Materials

For each picture:
Red plastic frame: 8,5 cm × 8,5 cm
14-count Aïda embroidery fabric: 14 cm square
DMC stranded embroidery cotton: 1 skein each 310, 699, 498, 743 and white. (This will be sufficient for both pictures.)
Embroidery needle
Embroidery frame
Wadding the same size as the inside of the picture frame

Method

○ Embroider the design (Sketch 32a or 32b) in the centre of the embroidery fabric.
○ Place the wadding on the card that fits inside the picture frame.
○ Place the embroidered motif on the wadding. Fold the extra fabric to the back and pull tightly. Sew the fabric together at the back.
○ Place the embroidery in the picture frame and seal the back.

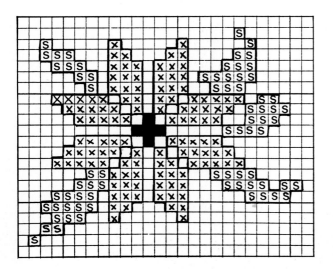

	DMC no.
S	699
X	498
■	743
W	white
For outlining – 310	

Sketch 32a

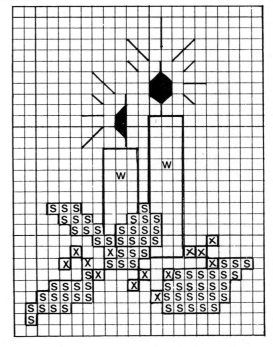

	DMC no.
S	699
X	498
■	743
W	white
For outlining – 310	

Sketch 32b

Christmas wreath

Materials

8 red silk poinsettias
20 green silk fern leaves
1 wreath-shaped oasis with a diameter of about 20 cm
16 mm wide dark green satin ribbon: 80 cm
1 florist's wire

Method

- Insert the fern leaves all the way round the oasis. Keep a few leaves for the opening in the centre.
- Insert the red silk flowers into the front of the oasis — space them so that the oasis does not show.
- Cut the florist's wire in half, bend one piece double and tie the satin ribbon in the loop. Insert the wire into the bottom curve of the wreath so that the ribbon hangs downwards.
- Use the remaining florist's wire to make a loop from which the wreath can be hung and secure it to the top of the wreath (Sketch 33).

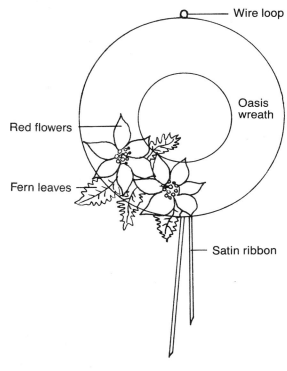

Sketch 33

Christmas stockings

Materials

For each stocking:
Red felt: 40 cm × 60 cm
White bias binding: 150 cm
Remnants of matching cotton fabric for decoration: 20 cm long (the width may vary as preferred)
3 cm wide white cotton lace: 20 cm
Green machine embroidery thread
Green and white sewing thread
Christmas bells and Christmas ribbon for decoration
Tracing paper

Method

- Trace Pattern 26 on p. 80 for the Christmas stocking. Lengthen the leg by 20 cm as shown on the pattern.
- Fold the red felt into two pieces, each 40 cm × 30 cm. Pin the pattern to the felt and cut it out.
- Finish off the two upper edges with bias binding.
- Decorate the front of the stocking with decorative stitches and strips of material and lace. Sew the bows and bells in place (see Sketch 34a and 34b).
- Place the front on the back with wrong sides facing and stitch together with a 5 mm seam.
- Bind the seam with white bias binding. Make sure that the ends are finished off very neatly.

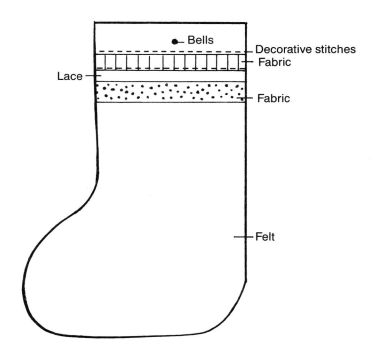

Sketch 34a

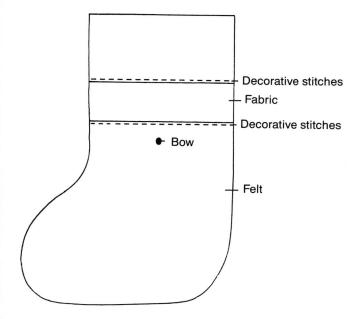

Sketch 34b

Christmas mouse

Materials

Unbleached linen for the head, ears and hands: 15 cm × 30 cm

Green cotton fabric with polka dots for the dress: 36 cm × 20 cm

Green cotton fabric with polka dots for the arms: 2 pieces, each 11 cm × 9 cm

White cotton fabric for the apron: 11 cm × 13 cm

Red cotton fabric with polka dots for the hat: circle with a diameter of 13 cm

Red cotton fabric with polka dots for the frill: 5 cm × 70 cm

2 cm wide lace for the apron and hat: 1 m

2,5 cm wide Christmas ribbon

Red, white and green sewing thread

Black felt for nose and eyes

A piece of white wire for spectacles

Glue

Filling

Silk flower for decoration

The top of a 2 litre cold drink bottle

Tracing paper

Method

○ Trace Pattern 27 on p. 80.
○ Cut out two pieces for the head from the unbleached linen. Place together with wrong sides facing and stitch from point A to point B. Clip where indicated and trim the seam at the tip of the nose (see Sketch 35a, point 1 and 2). Turn to the right side.
○ Gather the top edge of the fabric for the dress until it fits around the neck of the head section. With right sides facing, stitch the dress to the head.
○ Stitch the centre back seam of the dress from top to bottom.
○ Turn to the right side and stuff the head firmly to just above the neck seam. Pull the neck over the neck of the bottle, right down to the protruding edge (Sketch 35b, point 1).
○ Stitch a 1 cm casing at the bottom edge of the dress. Gather the casing with a needle and strong thread and pull very tightly. Sketch 35c shows how the dress now folds in around the opening of the bottle.
○ To make the arms, cut four hands from the unbleached linen. Place them together in pairs and, right sides facing, stitch each hand around the curve. Turn both to the right side.
○ Stitch the side seams of the two sleeves and, right sides facing and raw edges even, insert the hands into the sleeves (Sketch 35d). Gather the edges of the sleeves until they fit around the hands. Stitch the hands to the sleeves. Turn the sleeves to the right side and stuff both lightly.
○ Fold in 5 mm at the top raw edges of the sleeves. Tack the hem, pull the thread tightly and tie off. Sew the sleeves to the dress (Sketch 35e and 35f).
○ To make the apron, slightly round the two bottom corners of the white cotton fabric. Finish off the raw edges and stitch approximately 30 cm of the white lace around the edge of the apron (Sketch 35g). Fold over 5 mm at the top edge and gather the apron. Sew it onto the dress, about 1 cm under the neck seam.
○ Cut four ears from the unbleached linen. Place them together in pairs and, right sides facing, stitch each ear around the curve. Turn both ears to the right side. Turn in the raw edges and sew the opening closed by hand (Sketch 35h, point 1). Slipstitch the ears to the head.
○ Finish off the raw edges of the fabric for the hat. Gather the white lace into small pleats and stitch round the fabric circle.
○ Gather the hat around the outer edge and stuff lightly before sewing to the head.
○ Finish off both long sides of the red frill strip. Join the two ends, gather the frill evenly and glue it onto the hemline of the dress.
○ Tie the Christmas ribbon into a bow around the mouse's neck.
○ Cut two eyes and a nose from the black felt and glue to the face.
○ Redden the cheeks slightly with ordinary blusher.
○ Make the whiskers as follows: Tie a knot 1 cm from the one end in a length of thick, cream-coloured thread. Thread the other end through a needle and pull the thread through the mouse's nose. Tie a knot next to the fabric on the other side and cut 1 cm from the knot. Make three whiskers on each side (Sketch 35i).
○ Use the white wire to make the spectacles and sew in position.
○ Lastly sew the hands to the flowerstalk and voila! – the little mouse is ready to serve as a table decoration or gift.

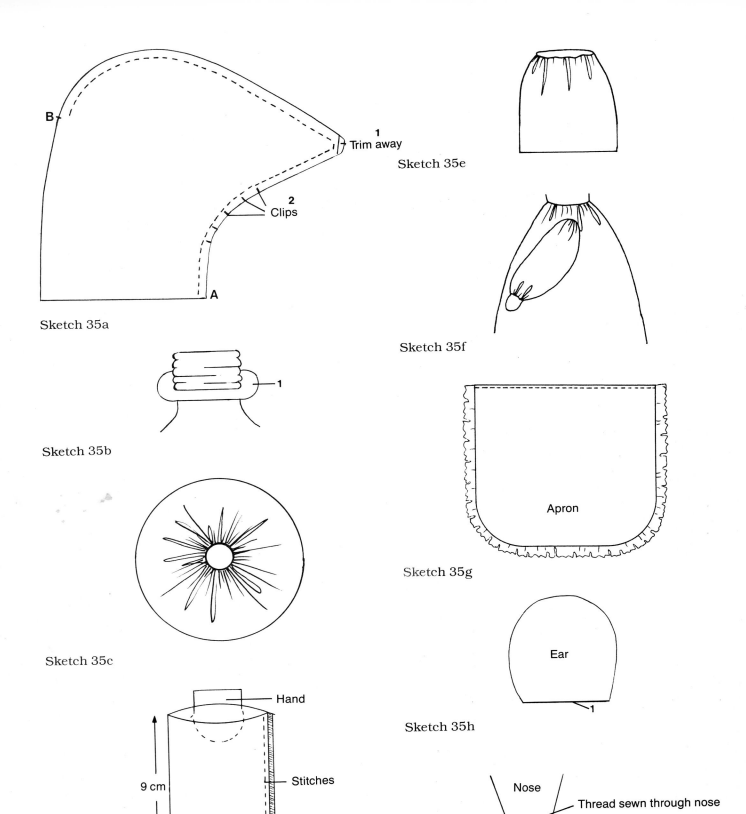

B

1
Trim away

2
Clips

A

Sketch 35a

Sketch 35e

1

Sketch 35b

Sketch 35f

Apron

Sketch 35g

Sketch 35c

Hand

9 cm

Stitches

Arm

Ear

1

Sketch 35h

Nose

Knot

Thread sewn through nose

Thread

Sketch 35d

Sketch 35i

Patterns

DMC-no.
A   913
B   910
o   742
•   Blanc
I   745
Lines on flowers – 762
Strawberries – 321
Stems – 913
White dots on strawberries – Blanc
Outlining of strawberries – 310
The lines on the diagram indicate the direction of the stitches

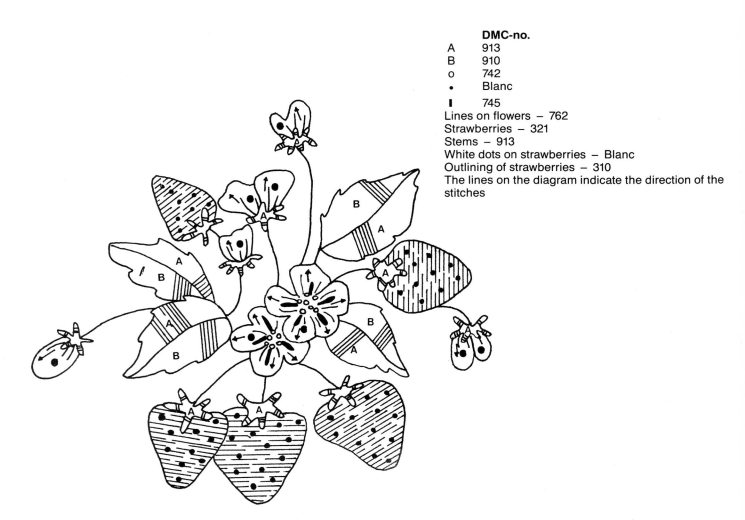

Pattern 1: Embroidery diagram for cushion with strawberry motif (p. 5)

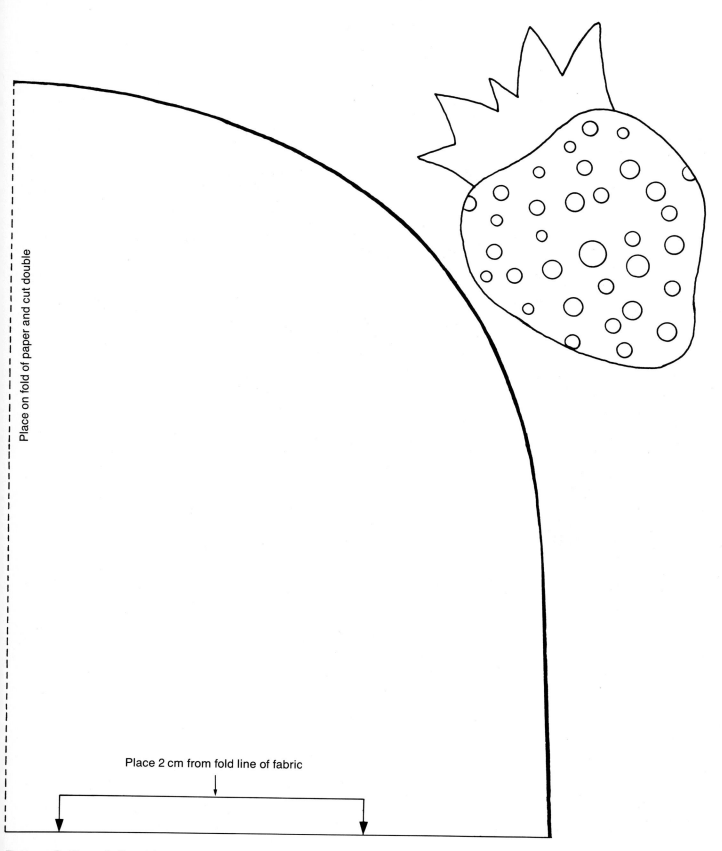

Pattern 2: Tray cloth with strawberry appliqué (p. 7). Also use this pattern for quilted tray cloth on p. 10 and the quilted place mat on p. 20.

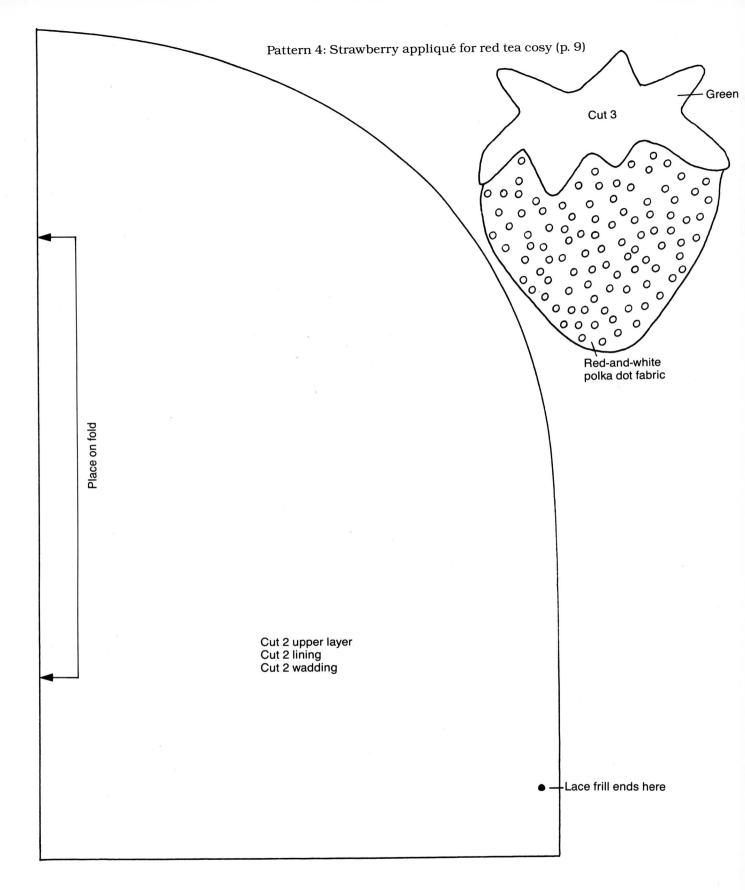

Pattern 4: Strawberry appliqué for red tea cosy (p. 9)

Green

Cut 3

Red-and-white
polka dot fabric

Place on fold

Cut 2 upper layer
Cut 2 lining
Cut 2 wadding

● Lace frill ends here

Pattern 3: Red tea cosy (p. 9)

58

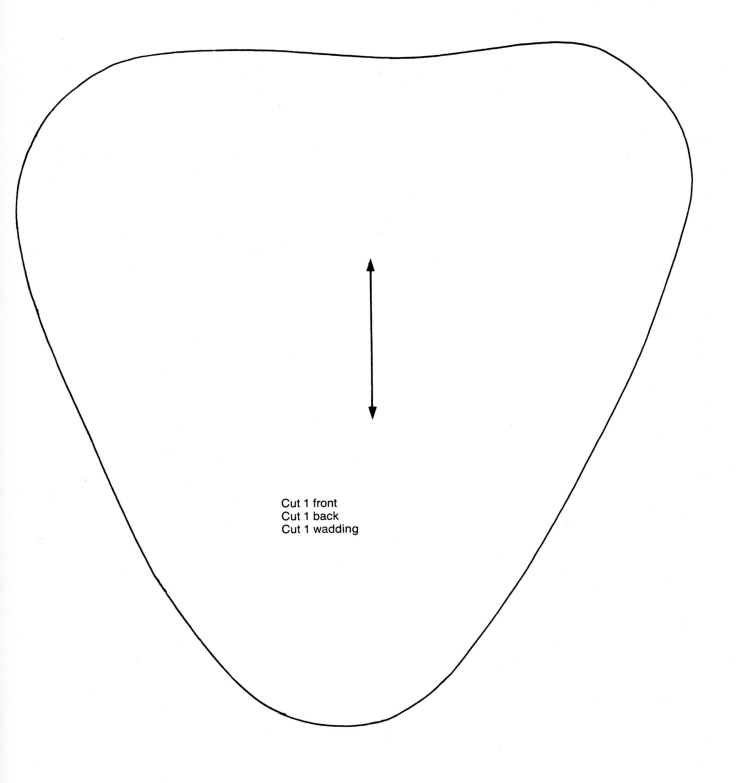

Cut 1 front
Cut 1 back
Cut 1 wadding

Pattern 5a: Strawberry pot-holder (p. 11)

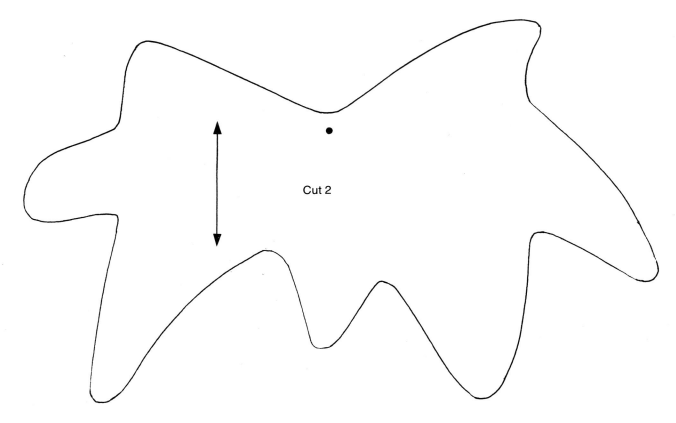

Cut 2

Pattern 5b: Strawberry pot-holder (p. 11)

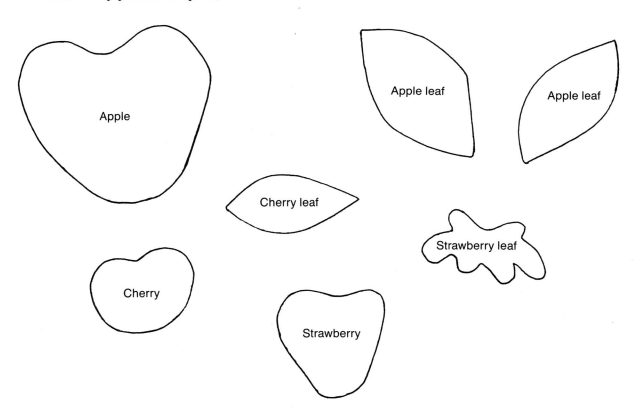

Apple

Apple leaf

Apple leaf

Cherry leaf

Strawberry leaf

Cherry

Strawberry

Pattern 6: Appliqué on jam jar covers (p. 13)

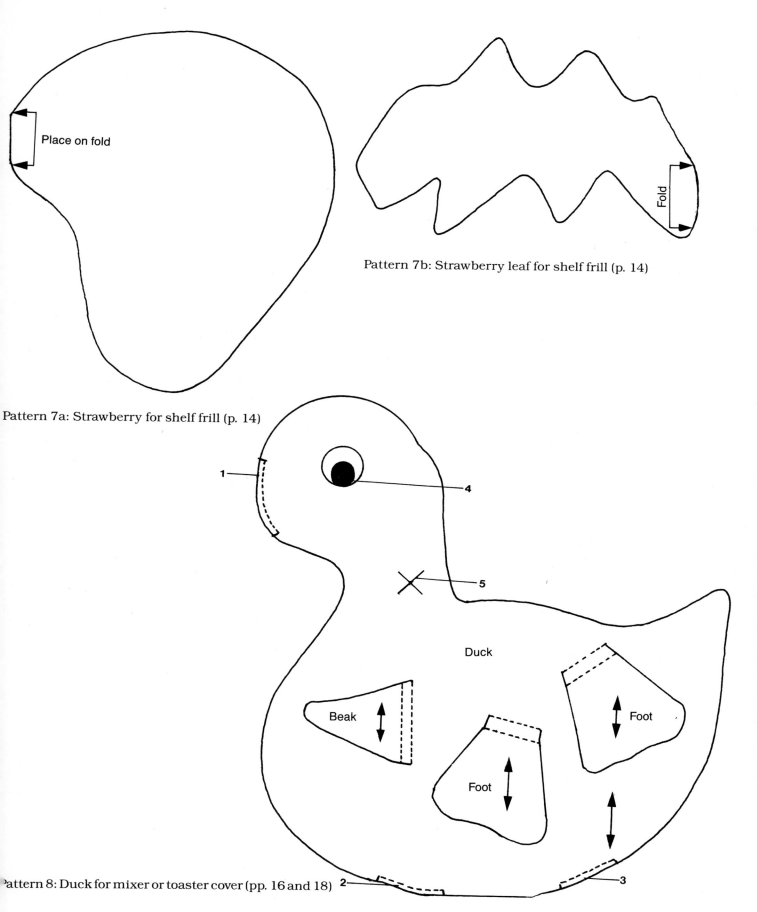

Place on fold

Pattern 7b: Strawberry leaf for shelf frill (p. 14)

Fold

Pattern 7a: Strawberry for shelf frill (p. 14)

1

4

5

Duck

Beak

Foot

Foot

Pattern 8: Duck for mixer or toaster cover (pp. 16 and 18)

2

3

61

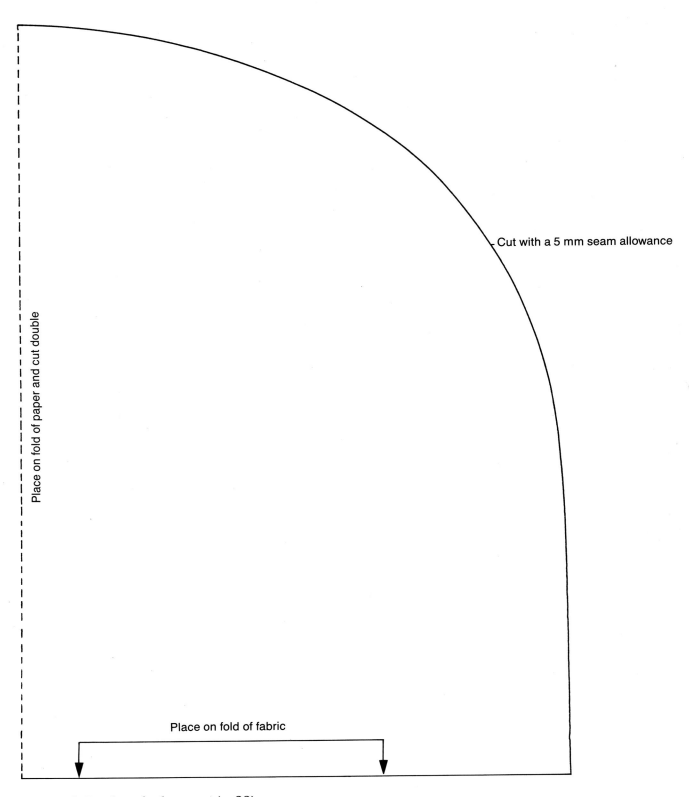

Place on fold of paper and cut double

Cut with a 5 mm seam allowance

Place on fold of fabric

Pattern 9: Patchwork place mat (p. 23)

Pattern 10: Paisley tea cosy (p. 23)

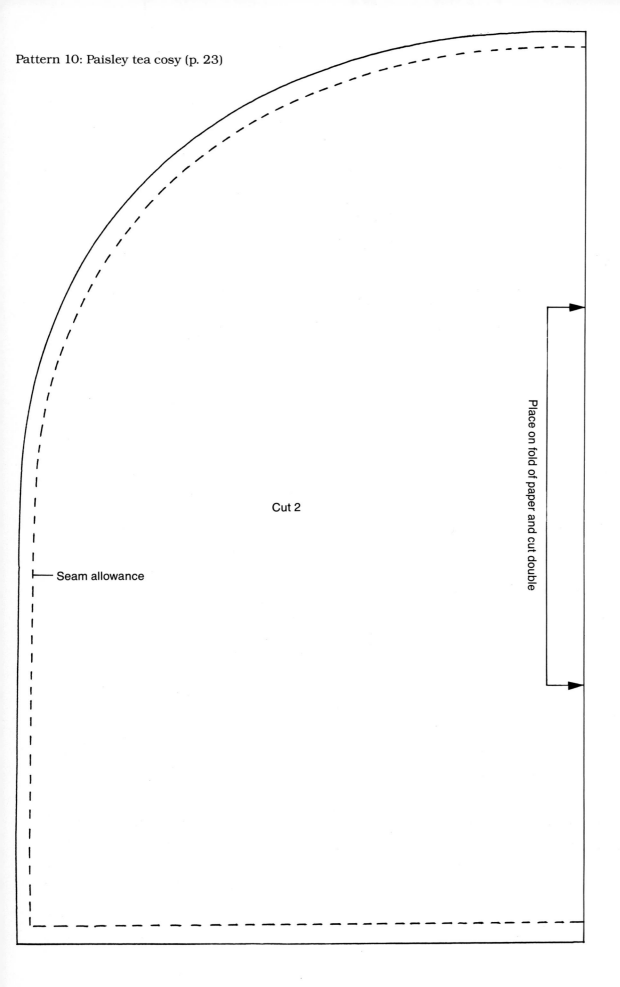

Cut 2

Seam allowance

Place on fold of paper and cut double

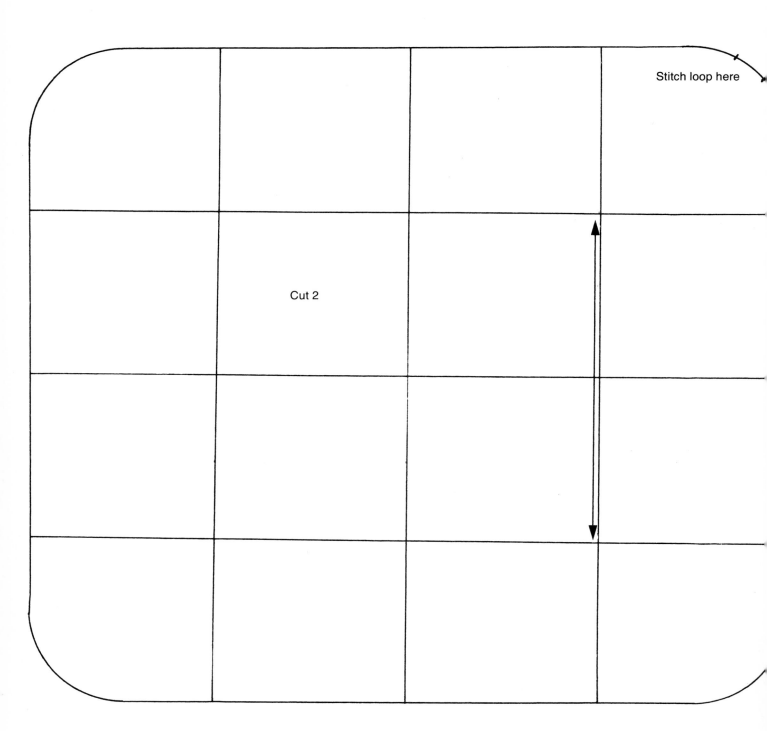

Stitch loop here

Cut 2

Pattern 11: Burgundy pot-holder (p. 24)

Pattern 12: Striped tea cosy (p. 26)

Place on fold of fabric

Frill starts here

Cut 2 outer layers

Cut 1 lining

Cut 1 thin foam or wadding

Pattern 13: Striped pot-holder (p. 26)

Pink

Salmon pink

Green

Burgundy

Dove blue

Lilac

Salmon pink

Pattern 14a: Parrot motif for cushion (p. 27)

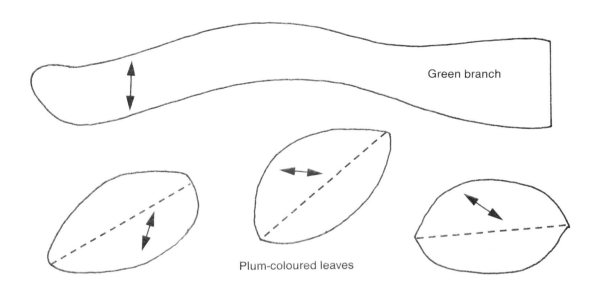

Green branch

Plum-coloured leaves

Pattern 14b: Parrot motif for cushion (p. 27)

	DMC-no.
A	758
B	948
C	334
D	522
o	543

The lines on the diagram indicate the direction of the stitches

Pattern 15a: Embroidery diagram for framed picture (p. 29)

Pattern 15b: Embroidery diagram for framed picture (p. 29)
See Pattern 15a for key

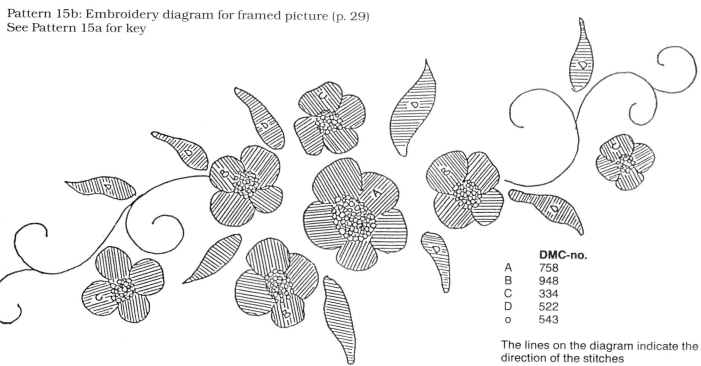

	DMC-no.
A	758
B	948
C	334
D	522
o	543

The lines on the diagram indicate the direction of the stitches

Pattern 16: Embroidery diagram for border of guest towel (p. 29)

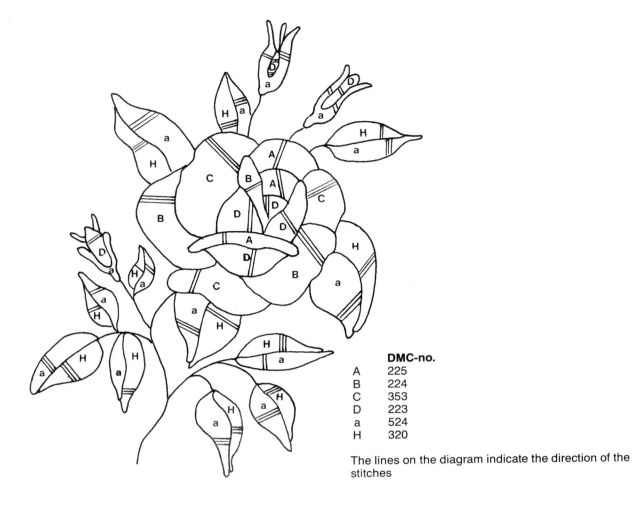

DMC-no.

A	225
B	224
C	353
D	223
a	524
H	320

The lines on the diagram indicate the direction of the stitches

Pattern 17: Embroidery diagram for cushion with rose motif (p. 31)

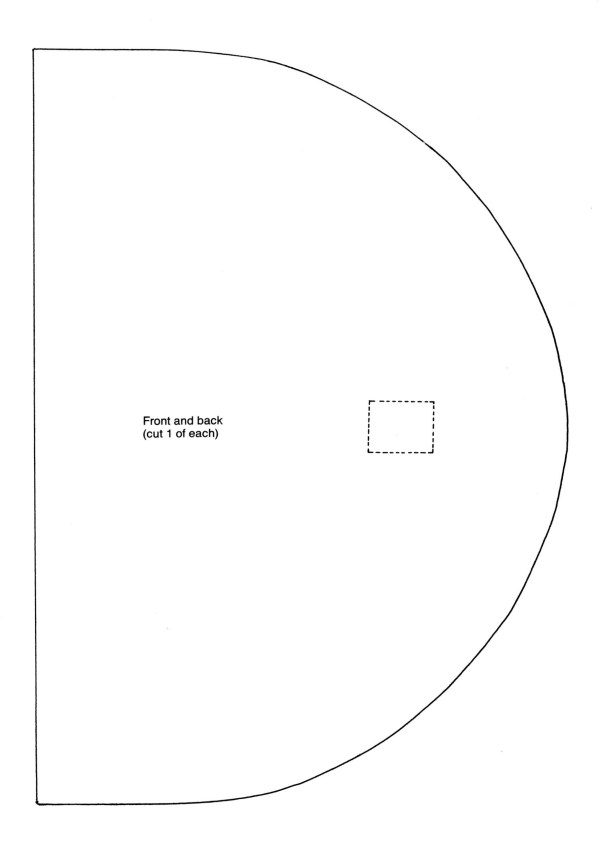

Front and back
(cut 1 of each)

Pattern 18a: Make-up bag (p. 34)

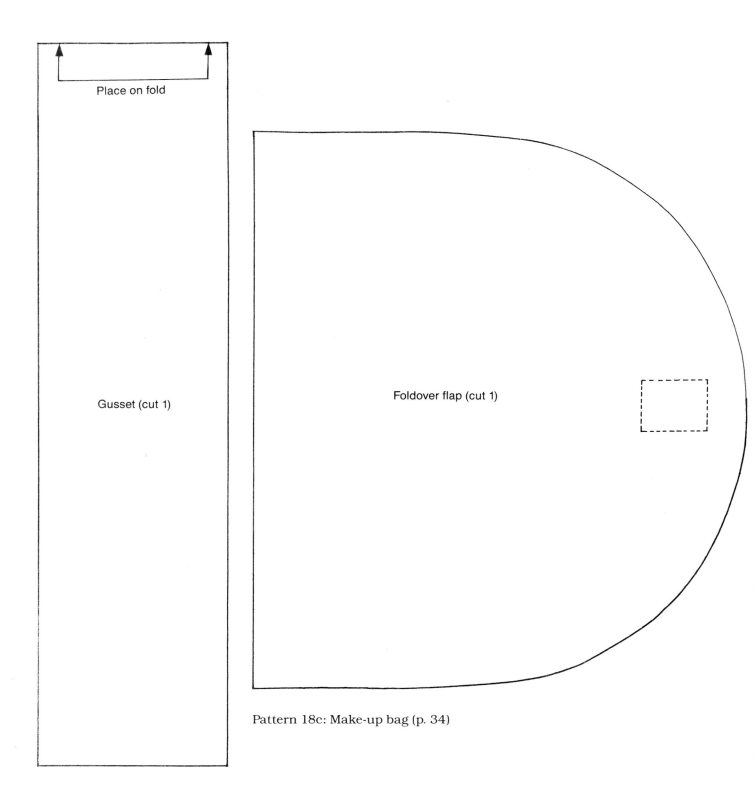

Place on fold

Gusset (cut 1)

Foldover flap (cut 1)

Pattern 18c: Make-up bag (p. 34)

Pattern 18b: Make-up bag (p. 34)

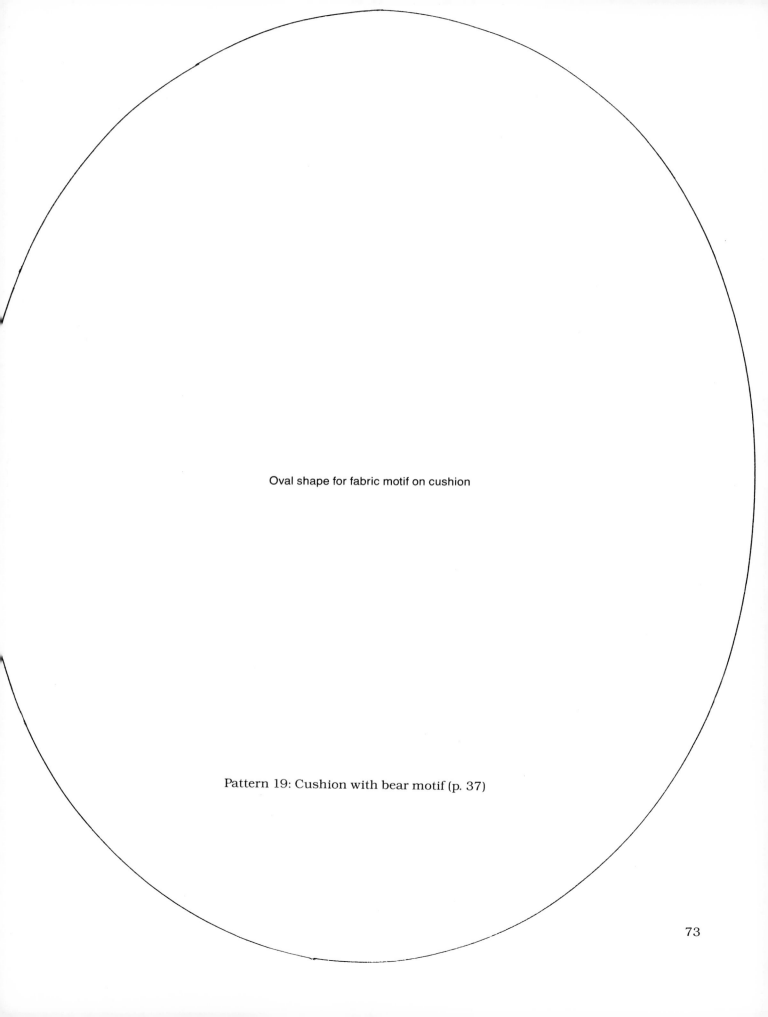

Oval shape for fabric motif on cushion

Pattern 19: Cushion with bear motif (p. 37)

Pattern 20: Clown motif for playpen blanket (p. 37)

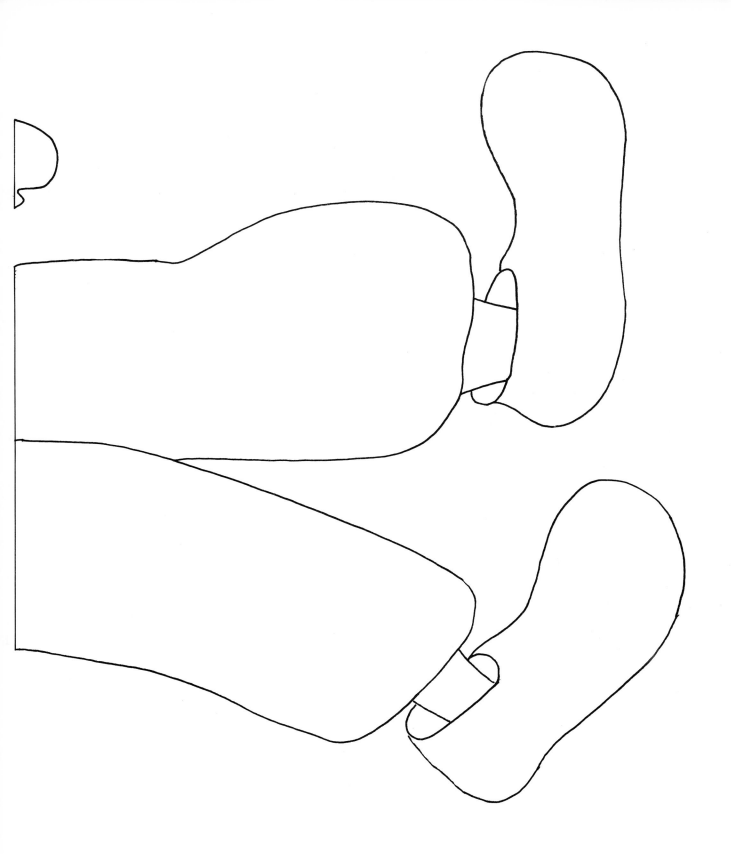

Pattern 20: Clown motif for playpen blanket (p. 37)

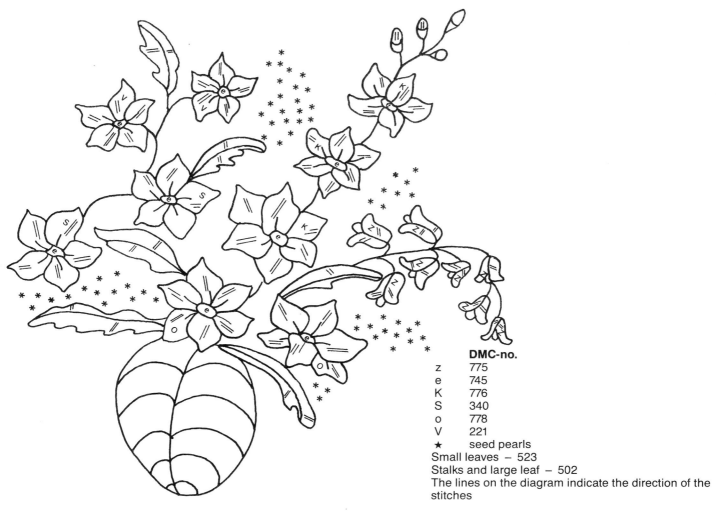

DMC-no.

z   775
e   745
K   776
S   340
o   778
V   221
★   seed pearls

Small leaves – 523
Stalks and large leaf – 502
The lines on the diagram indicate the direction of the stitches

Pattern 21: Embroidery diagram for framed picture and pink cushion (p. 44)

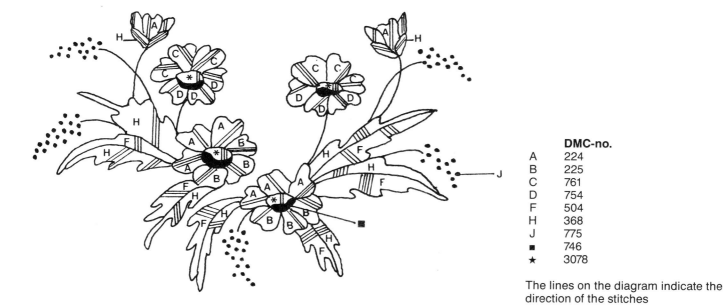

DMC-no.

A   224
B   225
C   761
D   754
F   504
H   368
J   775
■   746
★   3078

The lines on the diagram indicate the direction of the stitches

Pattern 22a: Embroidery diagram for cream cushion (p. 46)

Pattern 22b: Oval panel for cream embroidered cushion (p. 46)

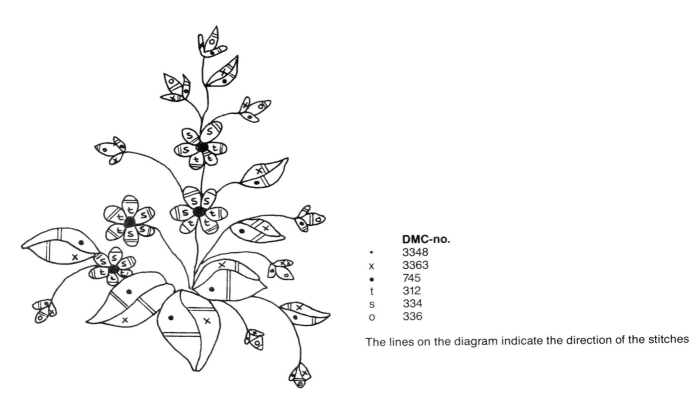

DMC-no.

•	3348
x	3363
●	745
t	312
s	334
o	336

The lines on the diagram indicate the direction of the stitches

Pattern 23: Embroidery diagram for blue-and-white cushion (p. 47)

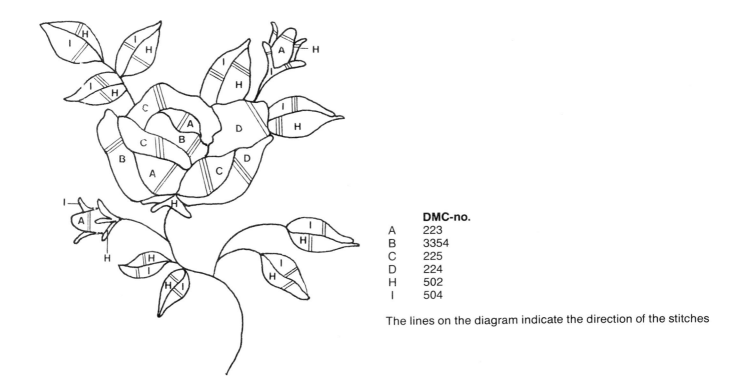

DMC-no.

A	223
B	3354
C	225
D	224
H	502
I	504

The lines on the diagram indicate the direction of the stitches

Pattern 24a: Embroidery diagram for white cushion (p. 48)

DMC-no.
★   225
D   224
E   316
a   369
s   368
●   seed pearl

The lines on the diagram indicate the direction of the stitches

Pattern 24b: Embroidery diagram for white cushion (p. 48)

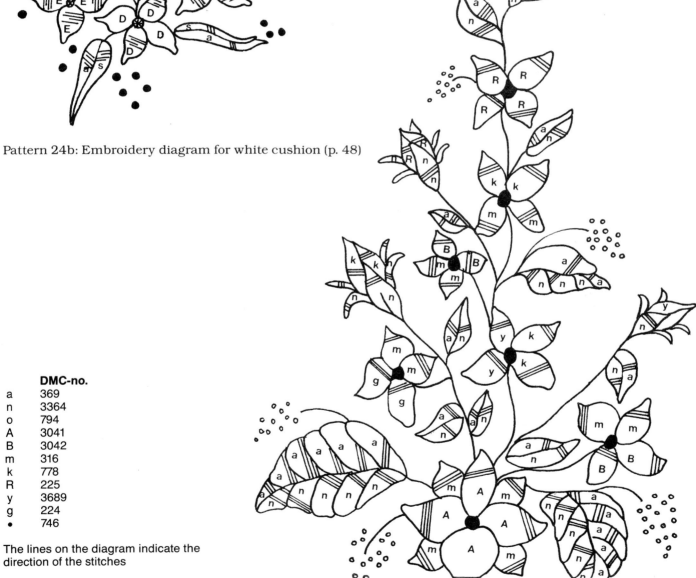

DMC-no.
a   369
n   3364
o   794
A   3041
B   3042
m   316
k   778
R   225
y   3689
g   224
●   746

The lines on the diagram indicate the
direction of the stitches

Pattern 25: Embroidery diagram for tablecloth (p. 49)

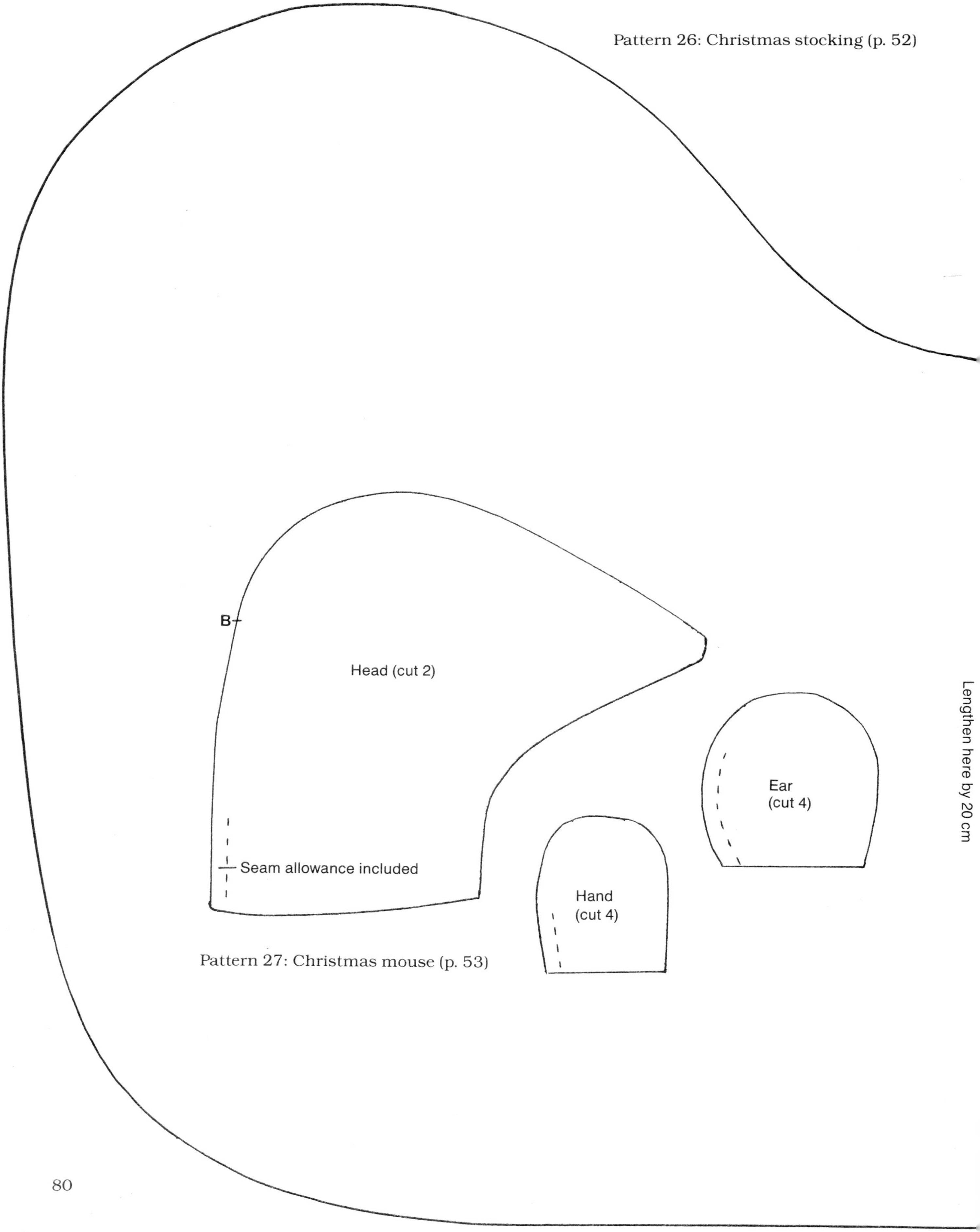

Pattern 26: Christmas stocking (p. 52)

B—

Head (cut 2)

— Seam allowance included

Pattern 27: Christmas mouse (p. 53)

Ear
(cut 4)

Hand
(cut 4)

Lengthen here by 20 cm